Alternatives To Tracking and Ability Grouping

BY ANNE WHEELOCK

NATIONAL UNIVERSITY
LIBRARY

AMERICAN ASSOCIATION OF SCHOOL ADMINISTRATORS

Related AASA Publications:

* *Building Self-Esteem*
* *Caught in the Middle: How To Unleash the Potential of Average Students*
* *An Effective Schools Primer*
* *Effective Teaching...Observations from Research*
* *Learning Styles*
* *The Nongraded Primary: Making Schools Fit Children*
* *Transforming Primary Schools To Improve Student Learning (audiocassettes)*

To order, call AASA's member/customer information line at (703) 875-0748.

© 1994, American Association of School Administrators
ISBN: 0-87652-199-5
Library of Congress Catalog Card No.: 94-72494
AASA Stock No.: 21–00447

CONTENTS

PREFACE

Tracking and ability grouping have become convenient ways of sorting students. However, when students are permanently placed in tracks or ability groups, they end up getting educationally richer or poorer.

For the high achieving student, placed in the "top" tracks or ability groups, expectations are high and the curriculum often is extra challenging. But for those students at the other end of the spectrum, expectations too often are lower and the curriculum is limited. When students are permanently isolated in tracks or ability groups, the gap in their learning and achievement widens with each day.

A number of respected school systems now are seeking alternatives to tracking and ability grouping, alternatives that will ensure an even better education for all students, whatever their abilities at any given point in time. After all, we have no students to waste.

Author Anne Wheelock is a widely published expert on tracking and ability grouping. Her highly acclaimed book, ***Crossing the Tracks: How "Untracking" Can Save America's Schools***, shook the foundations of America's education community and caused educators to think again about not only the effects but also the side effects of these longstanding techniques.

Alternatives To Tracking and Ability Grouping is designed to provide information, stimulate discussion, and motivate people to take action.

The most significant reform of our nation's schools directly and positively influences students in the classroom. This significant publication is sure to have a positive impact on the education and lives of educators and students everywhere.

Paul Houston
Executive Director
American Association of School Administrators

THE DAY I BECAME A BEAR

School had been uncomfortable for the first few years.
I had been told to speak in English and forget my Spanish.
I had become ashamed of my first language.
The teachers had drummed it into me, Spanish was bad and English was good.
By the third grade, I was reading very well in English
And had forgotten a great deal of my Spanish.
During the first week of school in the third grade, I was assigned to the Jets for Reading.
It was the very best reading group.
I was a Jet and I was soaring.
About a month into the year, the teacher
Asked me if I spoke Spanish at home.
I said yes.
The next day I became a Bluebird.
All of us knew the difference between a Jet and a Bluebird.
We knew it by the way the teacher treated us.
Jets were the best and the teacher loved the Jets.
Bluebirds were next and I had become one.
I felt bad that I could not stay a Jet.
I felt even worse that I did not know why
I could not stay a Jet.
Three months went by.
It was a cold day in February.
My mother who spoke no English had visited my teacher the previous week.
My teacher asked me about my life at home.
Don't you ever speak English at home?
No, I answered – My parents don't speak English at all.
Again, it was a cold day in February
When the teacher looked at me and said,
Today I am moving you to the Bears.
The Bears? I questioned. Why the Bears?
They are the lowest – the worst – the bottom.
Because you belong with the Bears.
In six short months, I went from a Jet to a Bear.
While I did not fully understand why I had become a Bear
I know, like every other Bear,
It was not the thing we wanted to be.
Why were there Jets, Bluebirds, and Bears?
Why couldn't everyone be a Jet?
While I didn't understand it
Quite as I understand it today
I began my real education
The day I became a Bear.

> – Peter J. Negroni,
>   Superintendent of Schools
>   Springfield, Massachusetts

INTRODUCTION

* In a midwestern town, a few high school teachers and a guidance counselor, tired of seeing too many students bored and turned off from learning, begin to question how their school's tracking and grouping practices alienate students.

* In a southwestern city school district, a team of sixth-grade teachers using active learning strategies in a heterogeneous humanities course successfully blend wealthy white suburban students with Latino students from the city's barrio. Poor students' test scores move from the lower percentiles into the middle range, while high-scoring students' test scores remain stable. The teachers wonder why their colleagues in subsequent grades can't adopt similar teaching and learning strategies.

* In a racially diverse suburb of a mid-Atlantic city, teachers and parents, concerned with intergroup relations in the district's schools, slowly discover that their schools' grouping practices have created a distinctly two-tiered education system. As these findings become public, the district's administrators are pushed to come up with alternatives to longstanding tracking practices, including pull-out special education and gifted classes, in the elementary schools.

* In a New England academic community, middle class African American and Latino parents question why their children are not represented in high school honors courses and why they are not enrolled in the middle school courses that lead to high level learning. Turning to a local attorney, these parents seek an answer in court.

Across the terrain of American public schools, some organizational practices are part of the background landscape, taken for granted, rarely questioned. Among these are practices that sort students into separate groups for teaching and learning according to their perceived academic capacity.

Over the past decade, however, more and more reformers have called for changes in rigid ability grouping and tracking, as these practices are called. Raising questions about the assumptions that undergird these practices, as well as their impact on student achievement, motivation, and aspirations, reformers say that tracking is not only harmful; it is no longer desirable or necessary.

This publication introduces practitioners to educators around the country who are developing alternatives to harmful grouping practices, with the goal of improving learning for all students. After a brief overview of the roots of sorting practices and how they shape teaching and learning, the book describes features of classrooms and schools that have begun to use heterogeneous groupings and other innovative classroom strategies. Finally, based on real school experiences, Chapters 3 and 4 describe the steps schools may take to replace traditional grouping practices with alternatives that encourage all students to learn at high levels.

W CHAPTER 1:
HAT IS TRACKING?

The terms tracking and ability grouping have narrow and broad definitions. In its traditional sense, tracking refers to the practice of sorting secondary school students into different programs of study, often called "college preparatory," "general," or "vocational." Ability grouping typically reflects similar sorting at the elementary and middle levels. It encompasses both "between-class" grouping, in which students are assigned to separate classes based on perceived ability, and "within-class" grouping in which smaller groups of students at similar performance levels work together in heterogeneous groups.

In practice, however, the distinction between tracking and between-class ability grouping is blurred. In many high schools, students enrolled in college preparatory or academic programs and classes may still be "leveled" into advanced, honors, standard, or basic courses, with students exposed to distinctly different curricula reflecting each label. In elementary and middle schools, students grouped in gifted, regular, or "low" classes frequently follow predictable paths into specific high school program tracks or levels. Consequently, many students, pegged in a low group early on, have few opportunities to learn or perform on an advanced level.

A broader view. This publication relies on a broad interpretation of tracking proposed by researcher Jeannie Oakes. Her landmark study, *Keeping Track: How Schools Structure Inequality,* offers the most extensive evidence that tracking greatly influences academic achievement, self-esteem, students' aspirations, teacher expectations, and the learning climate. As Oakes explains, in practice many educators use tracking and between-class ability grouping interchangeably to refer to practices that share two characteristics:

* A process involving educators' judgments of students' intellectual abilities or predictions of students' future accomplishment. These judgments lead to placing students with apparently similar abilities together in particular classes.

* Students in the different classrooms are exposed to different curricula and instruction.

Tracking, then, is about more than student grouping practices. It also touches on how schools allocate different learning experiences to different groups according to perceptions of their capacity to learn. Fortunately, the practice doesn't have to continue the way it has in the past. Teachers in schools that have rejected tracking and rigid ability grouping may use flexible and within-class groupings. These groupings are temporary, skill-specific, and designed to support students' success in heterogeneous classes that emphasize challenging curricula and instruction. However, success for all students will only happen through classroom innovations in teaching and learning and changes in school climate and routines.

How Are Tracked and Untracked Schools Different?

These are some common characteristics of traditional, tracked schools:

* Students are viewed as "having" a relatively fixed learning potential. "Smartness" is viewed as a scarce resource, with "smart" students identified according to measures of intelligence that place students across a bell-shaped curve.

* Students are sorted into classes based on their predicted futures, and educators view this task as part of their job.

* Student performance on "basic" school tasks, such as reading, writing, and computing, is valued as the most significant indicator of academic potential. Their performance is the basis for student groupings; both whole- and in-class groupings tend to be defined by "smartness" rankings in these areas. Students with disabilities receive "services" in a resource room.

* In classrooms, quick answers tend to be valued as the smartest answers. Some students may sit through entire class periods without interacting with either teachers or other students.

* Curriculum and instruction are tailored to the perceived ability of

Tracking, then, is about more than student grouping practices. It also touches on how schools allocate different learning experiences to different groups according to perceptions of their capacity to learn.

2

students. Curriculum frequently is "watered down" for students not labeled "gifted," or even "dumbed down" for below-average students.

* Teachers assign less challenging work to students who fall below a proficient academic level. Extra help is provided in place of "regular" classroom instruction.
* Opportunities for non-classroom learning, such as field trips, extracurricular activities, or student government, are distributed to the most "deserving" students first.
* Counselors match students with "appropriate" class levels.
* "Weighted grades" or "quality points" reinforce class rankings and grade point averages.

These are some features of untracked schools:

* All students are capable of learning at high levels and of developing a variety of skills, but they also need different amounts of time to master content.
* Understanding that all students need to be prepared for some kind of postsecondary education, educators provide opportunities for all students to learn about working in an increasingly multicultural society and technological economy.
* Persistence is valued over ability. Routines give students "second chances" and opportunities to improve on their "last best efforts."
* Divergent thinking and learning styles are respected. Multidimensional curricula and assignments to develop different learning intelligences are used.
* All students have equal access to knowledge in heterogeneous groups. Curriculum emphasizes thinking skills, and "basic skills" are embedded in complex project assignments.
* In-class groupings are flexible. Depending on the assignment, students with similar or different abilities may be grouped together. Student groupings vary over the year so all students work together at one time. Students with disabilities receive support in the "regular" classroom.
* Learning activities and assignments rely on many strategies that allow diverse learners to gain access to knowledge, understand content, and construct new knowledge. Interaction among students and teachers is all-inclusive.

* When students fall below levels of academic proficiency, teachers review their instructional approach and consider ways to mobilize extra resources and time to help them succeed in the challenging curriculum. Extra help is offered in addition to the "regular" class.
* Counselors work to create a strong academic climate for all students and to ensure all students receive support necessary to succeed in courses that will open doors to future opportunities.
* Assessments are multifaceted, performance-based, and criterion-referenced.

Roots of Sorting, Grouping, and Tracking Practices

Tracking only became a widespread practice in the 20th century. Throughout the 19th century, those children who attended school at all comprised a relatively homogeneous group of young scholars. Mostly white and middle class, these students experienced a common curriculum. If schools grouped students at all, they did so by age and grade, beginning only at the end of the century. As the middle class grew during the final decades of the 1800s, the school population grew as well. In response, the number of secondary schools expanded to accommodate them.

By the beginning of the 1900s, increasing numbers of immigrant families swelled the school rolls, especially in northeastern cities. The growing numbers of students attending public schools, including descendants of former slaves who had been excluded from school, coupled with the increasing economic and ethnic diversity of the student population, had created a dramatically new social context for schooling. These new conditions set the stage for a debate about the ends and means of public education that continues today in discussions about the purposes of grouping and tracking practices.

The debate begins

Though it picked up speed in the 1900s, the tracking debate formally started in 1892. The Committee of Ten, a panel of the National Education Association headed by Charles Eliot, president of Harvard University, focused on the growing number of secondary schools and the apparent need for programs to conform to college and university admission requirements. In its deliberations, the

Committee of Ten considered the goals of public education and asserted that all students in a democracy should have a broad and general education regardless of the adult roles they were likely to assume in society.

The Committee speculated that the numbers of students capable of studying geometry, algebra, and a foreign language probably were much greater than imagined. Believing that schools simply could not predict how students would use their education, Eliot and his colleagues proposed that secondary schools adopt an intellectually serious program for all — one that assumed college admission for every student via four different courses of study.

Opposition grows

Concerns About Heterogeneous Grouping

Although recent research questions the impact of tracking and ability grouping on students' school experiences, many educators and parents still have important concerns about untracking. Tracking supporters often raise these arguments:

* Tracking is both fair and accurate.
* High achievers are "held back" by slower students in heterogeneous classes.
* Slower students suffer from diminished self-esteem in mixed-ability groups.
* Teaching in heterogeneous classes is more difficult than in homogeneous classes because teachers have to deal with students' varying abilities.

Not all educators could accept either the Committee of Ten's premise or the recommendations in its report. To many, newcomers to American schools did not appear to have the intellectual promise of native-born students. Immigrants and other students, who usually spoke little English and were often poor and unhealthy, seemed less "fit" or "able" to use the knowledge schools had to offer. When early intelligence testing produced correlations between "low ability" and ethnic and racial differences, these observations seemed validated. Little or no consideration was given to how these students would have performed had they enjoyed the same advantages.

From that point, it was only a short step to conclude that individual differences required different programs of study for different groups of students according to their likely role in later life. Schools could offer something, but not the same thing, for everyone. If schooling could offer opportunities for some students to develop their intellectual potential, schooling for others could provide manual training and vocational education to socialize them into their future roles as industrial workers.

Many tracks develop

By the mid-1920s, some high school programs included as many as eight different tracks representing differing expectations for students: classical, arts, engineering, academic, normal, commercial business, commercial secretarial, and general. This multitiered differentiation reflected a compromise between those who believed all students could benefit from a secondary school education to develop their intellectual skills and those who held that such an education was wasted on students who were destined for factory or manual labor. Separate tracks, labeled to mirror students' predicted futures, institutionalized the belief that some students were better equipped than others to benefit from access to certain knowledge.

Academic versus vocational. Over the rest of the 20th century, sorting and grouping practices became increasingly elaborate, but not in a uniform way. Most common was the sorting of students into academic and vocational programs, including agricultural schools. But for decades, many small schools, including private secular, religious, and public schools, especially in rural areas, simply did not have the resources to offer a wide variety of programs under one roof.

Only in the 1960s, when many districts moved to consolidate small schools into comprehensive high schools, did students from smaller communities receive curriculum and instruction differentiated according to apparent academic ability, often assessed by standardized tests. And only after the Sputnik launching of 1957 seemed to suggest that American students were not scientifically competitive with their Soviet counterparts did schools receive additional resources to strengthen programs for top-scoring students — sometimes called "gifted and talented" students. However, little comparable attention was paid to enriching learning for all students.

More diversity, more groups

During the 1960s and 1970s, the increasingly diverse student population again invited further curriculum differentiation and often separation of groups of students within public schools. New Chapter 1 programs, as well as special education and bilingual education programs, expanded access to public schools to many students who had not been attending school at all.

But while students with disabilities, second-language learners, and economically disadvantaged children entered school buildings in record numbers, their learning programs often segregated them from "mainstream" students, further fragmenting the student population. Special education and Chapter 1 programs are not always considered along with traditional tracks. However, they do assess and label students as well as provide different curricula to different groups — often based on lower expectations. For these reasons, they are part of the operating tracking system.

A Widespread Practice

As American schools reassess how well they are preparing all students for the 21st century, sorting and tracking practices remain common in the 1990s. For example:

* At the elementary level, whole- or between-class ability grouping and pull-out programs often are the approach of choice for students enrolled in Chapter 1, special education, and gifted and talented programs. Researcher Jeannie Oakes estimates that approximately 60 percent of all elementary schools still use some form of between-class ability grouping.

* In the middle grades, a 1993 study by the National Association of Secondary School Principals reports that ability grouping in separate classes exists in 82 percent of their schools, with 72 percent of teachers in school leadership teams favoring such between-class grouping.

* Researchers Jomills Braddock of the University of Miami and Robert Slavin of Johns Hopkins University in Baltimore, Maryland, report that although whole-class ability grouping is less widespread in the fifth and sixth grades, the percentage of classes that are grouped by ability increases as students proceed into ninth grade. According to their 1993 analysis of the National Educational Longitudinal Study of 1988 (NELS:88), the percentage of young adolescent students grouped homogeneously for math increases every year, growing from 57 percent in fifth grade to 94 percent in ninth grade.

* By eighth grade, different groupings represent distinctly different levels of access to knowledge. For example, the 1990 National

Assessment of Educational Progress reports that while 58 percent of eighth-graders are enrolled in "eighth-grade mathematics, which focuses on numbers and operations," 22 percent are in pre-algebra, and 16 percent are taking algebra.

✳ In high schools, Jeannie Oakes estimates that approximately 80 percent of all schools offer tracks in which homogeneously grouped classes of students receive distinctly different learning experiences.

As familiar as tracking is, however, the practice may no longer suit the changing social conditions and demands of the approaching 21st century.

Basing Change on Reality

Tracking and ability grouping is grounded in the habits and realities of America's schools and communities. As Paul George, author of numerous articles and reports on tracking and ability grouping has noted, many teachers are not prepared for heterogeneously grouped classes and find them more difficult to teach. In some schools, parents of children grouped in the top levels are well organized to oppose changes in practices they believe benefit their children.

These sources of resistance suggest that introducing alternatives requires knowledge of teaching strategies that work with multiability groups, an understanding of the political dimensions of school reform, and a willingness to reconsider outmoded beliefs about learning.

Undesirable and unnecessary. The conditions that support tracking and rigid ability grouping have prevented many educators from moving toward alternatives, even when they are not entirely comfortable with sorting students into "high" and "low" groups. However, changing expectations for schooling, a new understanding of alternatives to ability grouping, and solid research findings now support the intuition that tracking might not be the best practice for all students. Based on a deepening understanding of learning theory and a commitment to provide equal access to the best schooling they can offer, some educators are boldly demonstrating that tracking is both undesirable and unnecessary.

W CHAPTER 2:
HY DEVELOP ALTERNATIVES?

A fter 70 years of widespread use, homogeneous grouping is coming to be seen as increasingly unnecessary. Recent research has clarified the largely negative impact of tracking on student achievement and motivation. In its place, innovative educators have developed effective strategies for multiability grouping of students at all levels. At the same time, professional and community organizations have taken public stands against tracking, resulting in pressure from both policymakers and the courts for schools to develop alternatives that can bring about higher achievement and improved learning climates for all students.

Research Questions Fairness and Accuracy

C laims that homogeneous grouping practices are fair and accurately reflect a student's learning potential simply do not hold up under scrutiny. For example, in a 1993 analysis of a multiethnic district of white, Latino, and Asian students, researcher Jeannie Oakes found that in practice all ability groups — high, average, and low — include students whose test scores range from the lowest to the highest percentiles. When she compared students with the same test scores, she found dramatic ethnic differences in placement by ethnicity, with white students 70 percent more likely than Latinos, and Asian students more than twice as likely as Latinos, to be placed in accelerated courses.

Tracking and minority students

In tracked schools, African American and Latino students typically are missing from top-level classes. Conversely, according to 1988 data reported by Jomills Braddock when he was at Johns Hopkins University in Baltimore, Maryland, African American, Latino, Native American, and low-income eighth-graders are twice as likely as white or upper-income eighth-graders to be in remedial math courses.

Moreover, Oakes and colleagues from the RAND Corporation report that districtwide tracking practices result in entire schools dominated by a remedial curriculum — effectively denying many poor, African American, Latino, and recent immigrant students the opportunity to acquire higher level knowledge. In schools with large African American and Latino enrollments (50 percent or more), advanced classes make up only 12 percent of math and science offerings. In comparison, in schools with an enrollment of 50 percent or more white students, advanced classes comprise 34 percent of all math and science courses.

These and other data from district-based studies suggest that all students simply do not have the same opportunities for success from school to school. Students who are not challenged academically are less motivated to learn in general. Depressed achievement inevitably results from schooling that offers students few courses above a remedial level.

> *Recent learning theory also questions the assumption that a student's capacity to learn is fixed and unchangeable.*

New intelligence theories

Recent learning theory also questions the assumption that a student's capacity to learn is fixed and unchangeable. In fact, young people experience continual cognitive growth at all ages. The depth and extent of their development depends a great deal more on the academic challenges schools offer than on native ability. Nor is intelligence an attribute that can be measured in linear ways.

Instead, researchers increasingly are drawn to Howard Gardner's multidimensional approach to intelligence. Gardner, a psychologist and professor of education at Harvard University, suggests that human beings are capable of developing seven different ways of knowing the world: verbal-linguistic, logical-mathematical, kines-

thetic, musical, visual, intrapersonal, and interpersonal. These concepts of intelligence question traditional measures of aptitude as well as the habit of using these measures to shape educational opportunity in public schools.

Impact on Achievement and Self-Esteem

Most responsible studies find that tracking and ability grouping do not produce gains in student achievement, especially among students placed below the top levels. In fact, lower scoring students achieve at even slower rates in homogeneous classes. These same students, when placed in heterogeneous classes, perform at higher levels and experience greater opportunity in their later schooling.

For example, researchers Braddock and Slavin made an interesting discovery from their review of the most recent follow-up data of the 1988 National Educational Longitudinal Study survey of 25,000 students: Students placed in heterogeneous classes in eighth grade were performing significantly better in tenth grade than their counterparts who had been in homogeneous classes (controlled for prior grades, test scores, ethnicity, income level, and other variables).

In addition, the heterogeneously grouped eighth-graders were far more likely to be in college preparatory classes in the tenth grade, and high achievers in heterogeneous eighth grades performed at equally high levels two years later. Based on such evidence, the researchers concluded the overall drawbacks of homogeneous grouping far outweighed any net gain. Conversely, the benefits of heterogeneous groups outweigh the negatives.

Low expectations, low self-esteem. Student self-esteem suffers considerably in the lower tracks. Contrary to popular assumptions, homogeneous grouping does not benefit slower students' self-perception or their sense of control over learning. As students conclude that their low grouping and less challenging curriculum accurately reflect the school's assessment of their abilities, they become increasingly less motivated to make the effort necessary for learning.

Students at lower levels look around and see themselves grouped with others who have been sorted according to the same low expectations. Not surprisingly, when these groups include students placed together "for behavioral reasons," teachers often must spend as much time controlling students as teaching them. In turn, this response reinforces students' image of themselves as inadequate learners.

Curtailed access to advanced instruction

Students placed at different levels have distinctly different levels of access to knowledge, a major factor contributing to unequal learning outcomes. As many researchers have reported, students grouped at the top are much more likely to receive instruction that develops critical thinking, depth of knowledge, and practice in problem solving and applying learning to create new information and knowledge. Students at the top also are more likely to experience hands-on science learning, math applications, research assignments, and opportunities to read and discuss challenging literature. In contrast, students at the bottom often are grouped in classes that emphasize rote learning, basic skills-oriented review, and fragments of literature.

Not only do students in remedial settings receive a less demanding curriculum but they're also more likely to have teachers with less classroom experience. As Lorraine McDonnell and her RAND Corporation colleagues discovered in their 1990 research, teachers in 42 percent of the remedial, vocational, and general mathematics sections studied had been teaching for five years or less, compared with only 19 percent of the teachers in pre-algebra and Algebra 1 sections.

Inflexible grouping placements

Some tracking supporters argue, despite critics' claims, that tracking does not prevent students from moving up when they are ready for more challenging work. However, close scrutiny of ability grouping and tracking in practice reveals that students are more likely to move down than up.

In *A Place Called School*, the first of a three-volume study of schooling released in the 1980s, John Goodlad reviewed grouping practices at all levels. He found that regrouping for reading and math instruction was rare after the first few months of the first grade. As he explains:

> One of the reasons for this stability in group membership is that the work of upper and lower groups becomes more sharply differentiated with each passing day. Since those comprising each group are taught as a group most of the time, it is difficult for any one child to move ahead and catch up with children in a more advanced group, especially in mathematics.

Unintentionally, then, early ability groupings reinforce later tracking. As the "slow" students move more slowly through a sequential curriculum, they almost inevitably come to seem less "ready" for the more challenging material at the secondary level. With some students offered more enriched learning activities than others, early differences in learning become more pronounced. Placing different groups of students in settings that offer still more differentiated levels of curriculum and instruction comes to seem inevitable.

Effects on students' interest in learning

Tracking and ability grouping adherents sometimes argue that high achieving students are bored in heterogeneous classes and that "teaching to the middle" decelerates the learning of above-average students.

The reality is that most students, those in traditional tracks and otherwise, appear bored and disengaged in school. John Goodlad has observed that boredom is "epidemic" in most American schools. Likewise, in **Inside Grade Eight**, a 1990 study for the National Association of Secondary School Principals, researchers John Lounsbury and Donald Clark estimate that half of all eighth-graders are bored more than 50 percent of their time in school. These figures suggest that many learners, regardless of their ability level, are not academically challenged in school. The findings highlight the importance of engaging all students in long-term projects, meaningful primary research, and hands-on, experiential activities that promote in-depth learning and individual growth.

A learning environment that is both challenging and nurturing is the most critical ingredient to success for all students.

Environment counts. A learning environment that is both challenging and nurturing is the most critical ingredient to success for all students. When students interact in this type of environment, they engage in meaningful assignments, analyze and synthesize information, and test new hypotheses. In such classrooms, teachers value divergent thinking and use the ideas and observations students generate as the basis for further learning. These settings are heterogeneous classrooms, and they are "achieving classrooms" that benefit everyone.

Lessons from Recent Reform Movements

During the 1980s and 1990s, several coalitions of educators and reformers emerged to provide a context for reconsidering traditional sorting and tracking practices — drawing both from recent research and the philosophy of Charles Eliot and the Committee of Ten. These coalitions continue to support alternatives to tracking through networks of educators and resource banks of innovative teaching and learning strategies for heterogeneous groups.

Many untracking schools identify with the principles embodied in one or more of these movements and have revised their beliefs and techniques to reflect them:

* Henry Levin's Accelerated Schools Project at Stanford University, which builds on student strengths.
* Theodore Sizer's Coalition of Essential Schools at Brown University, which is committed to a core curriculum and continuity of student-teacher relationships.
* John Goodlad's Partnership for School Renewal, dedicated to aligning school practices with research findings.
* Paideia schools, inspired by Mortimer Adler's Paideia Proposal, which focus on the virtues of a single-track liberal arts curriculum.

Theory into practice

Schools that identify with well-known reform principles frequently choose to replace harmful grouping practices with high level educational opportunities for all students in multiability groups. For example:

* The Burnett Academy in San Jose, California, was heavily tracked, especially in language arts, social studies, and mathematics, when educators embraced the philosophy of the Accelerated Schools Network in 1990. School staff first assessed the school's enrollment patterns in particular courses, then created

a school vision, and reexamined curriculum and instruction in light of research by staff members and committees.

Later, as teachers experimented with heterogeneously grouped classes, they also became more committed to giving all students equal access to valued curricula.

* As a member of the Coalition of Essential Schools, Castle High School in Kaneohe, Hawaii, adopted the Coalition's Nine Common Principles to introduce a core curriculum focused on student mastery and achievement in all ninth- and tenth-grade classes. School goals apply to all students. Rather than accommodate students in less demanding courses, scheduling changes are made to support those who need extra time and help to succeed in the core curriculum.

* As a school participating in John Goodlad's Partnership for School Renewal, the Middle School of the Kennebunks in Kennebunkport, Maine, has adopted increasingly research-based practices. Staff regularly examine their practices against research findings. As a result, the school has come to consider issues related to student grouping and access to knowledge.

Over time, teachers have worked slowly to develop a solid, interdisciplinary curriculum with expanded access for all. Student clusters are all grouped heterogeneously, with flexible grouping the norm in most classrooms.

* In Chattanooga, Tennessee, two Paideia schools, the Chattanooga School for the Arts and Sciences and the Chattanooga School for Liberal Arts, are models for offering all students high level curriculum and instruction in heterogeneous classes.

Based on a belief that public schools should prepare all children for citizenship, work, and lifelong learning in a democracy, these schools offer a challenging, single-track, liberal arts curriculum to all. In the wake of their success, the district has moved to support three other schools — one elementary, one middle, and one high school — as they shift from homogeneously grouped classes to multiability groups.

Like other schools affiliated with larger reform movements, the schools described above benefit from support networks and movements beyond their district as they replace harmful tracking practices with high level, heterogeneous educational opportunities.

Economic Realities

Tracked schools evolved in tandem with an industrial economy that rested on a hierarchical workplace. As the United States approaches the 21st century, the assembly line is becoming a thing of the past. The American economy is relying more and more on workers who can work with others to solve complex problems. Moreover, future workers can expect to change occupations several times during their lifetimes.

Given these economic changes, schools must reshape their expectations for students. Today, all students should be prepared for postsecondary education to be competitive in the marketplace. They must have experience working with peers of diverse backgrounds. Above all, the economy of the next century will favor lifelong learners who know how to apply learning in new areas. These imperatives require schooling that expands students' access to higher level curricula in heterogeneous groups.

The Public Calls for Change

As educators and citizens learn about research findings related to tracking and understand the potential of alternatives to improve outcomes for all students, a growing number of professional and educational organizations have called publicly for an end to tracking and rigid ability grouping. Their conclusions reflect a growing consensus that schools must offer all students equal access to valued knowledge and restructure educational opportunities to reflect high expectations for all learners.

Higher standards

Across the country, educators, policymakers, and legislators are calling for higher standards. They say all students, regardless of where they are educated, should be able to demonstrate mastery of certain kinds of knowledge as well as to synthesize, organize, and apply this knowledge to complex problems.

Several professional associations, with the National Council of Teachers of Mathematics in the lead, have formulated standards for learning in their own disciplines. An independent commission on Chapter 1 also has proposed steps to ensure that all students will learn at high levels. Spurred by national policy, many states are formulating expected learner outcomes that emphasize the need for all children to acquire learning for the 21st century.

Given these economic changes, schools must reshape their expectations for students. Today, all students should be prepared for postsecondary education to be competitive in the marketplace.

Current tracking and ability grouping practices cannot exist side by side with higher expectations for all students. As the National Governors' Association points out, "It will be difficult, perhaps impossible, to raise achievement levels for middle- and low-achieving students without addressing current grouping practices."

Court cases and community challenges

In some districts, community dissatisfaction with sorting and ability grouping practices has led to legal disputes on curriculum and tracking issues. Several court decisions related to district reorganization or desegregation have addressed tracking concerns. For example, in 1993:

❋ Court desegregation orders yielded curriculum revisions in Rockford, Illinois, including elimination of basic and remedial classes, enrollment of all seventh-graders in pre-algebra courses, and elimination of reading-level requirements for foreign language study in the eighth grade.

U.S. Magistrate Judge P. Michael Mahoney found that tracking and ability grouping locked minority students into lower track classes, leaving them with little or no hope of ever moving upward. The district has agreed to increase the percentage of

African American and Latino students in gifted programs and ensure that honors courses are racially balanced.

* Plaintiffs in a local desegregation case in San Jose, California, sought to keep the case open until the district reformed ability grouping and tracking practices that segregated Latino students within schools and excluded them from the district's most valued learning opportunities. As a result, the school district is working with the Accelerated Schools Network to reform many of its grouping practices.

* A court remedy order issued to shape Alabama's education reform reads: "Schools shall not track students, relegate particular students to a general track of undemanding courses, or design coursework that forecloses educational and occupational options. Programs shall not result in de facto tracking and shall include safeguards to ensure that factors such as socioeconomic status, race, gender, and disability do not limit or determine students' post-high school pursuits."

Current tracking and ability grouping practices cannot exist side by side with higher expectations for all students.

In each scenario, citizens turned to the courts to pressure school districts to develop alternatives to tracking. The cases set precedents for what other communities can expect their schools to offer all students.

National education associations respond

Professional education groups across the country also have vocally opposed tracking and ability grouping. For example:

* From the Council for Basic Education *(Off the Tracks)*:

No single widespread practice in American schools is as pernicious, is as counter to the philosophy of the Council for Basic Education as the systematic and rigid grouping of students into separate educational "tracks" according to supposed aptitude. Poor and minority students pay an especially high price, for they are the ones most often herded into less challenging, less fulfilling, and less empowering tracks. Unless we demolish the tracks themselves, other reforms in our schools will be derailed.

* From the Education Commission of the States *(Current Practice: Is It Enough?):*

  Student assignment and grouping patterns tend to lock [disadvantaged students] into [inadequate learning] environments, confining them to their peer group and depriving them of interaction with a diversity of students and exposure to other views.... Without a change in how curriculum and the school day are organized, accompanied by changes in instructional strategies and student grouping arrangements, it is unlikely that [other] changes will increase student achievement, especially for those who need it most.

* From the National Governors' Association *(Ability Grouping and Tracking):*

  Current ability grouping and tracking practices perpetuate low levels of performance for average and below-average students. In addition, these practices tend to maintain low expectations, especially for minority students.... It is doubtful that the performance of American students, and especially those students relegated to the general track in high schools or low-level groups in elementary school, can be improved significantly with current ability grouping and tracking practices. If students are sorted out of opportunities to succeed or are unnecessarily labeled or categorized, then efforts geared toward systemic educational reform will be hampered.

* From the Carnegie Council on Adolescent Development *(Turning Points: Preparing American Youth for the 21st Century):*

  Tracking is one of the most divisive and damaging school practices in existence.... Time and again, young people placed in lower academic tracks or classes, often during the middle grades, are locked into dull, repetitive instructional programs leading at best to minimum competencies. The psychic numbing these youth experience from a "dumbed-down" curriculum contrasts sharply with the exciting opportunities for learning and critical thinking that students in the higher tracks or classes may experience.

* From the National Commission on Secondary Schooling for Hispanics *("Make Something Happen:" Hispanics and Urban High School Reform):*

John Goodlad, in **A Place Called School**, recom-
mends the elimination of tracking at all levels of
schooling. We concur, and we agree with another
recent report that "the education needed for the
workplace does not differ in its essentials from that
needed for college or advanced training".... Excellence must not
be an absolute standard, but the opportunity to strive for excellence must be available to all and inclusive of everyone.

* From the Quality Education for Minorities Project *(Education
That Works: An Action Plan for the Education of Minorities):*

[We recommend that schools] eliminate ability grouping and age
grading in the elementary grades. The decision about how to

track a new student rarely takes more than a week; the
damage lasts a lifetime. School boards should require
principals and teachers to address differential rates of
preparation for learning by such techniques as flexible
pacing and cooperative learning, not by segregating
students according to the artificial criteria of precon-
ceived expectations and often suspect tests.... On the
larger scale, we strongly support the development of a core
academic curriculum for middle and senior high school students
that prepares all students for college or a meaningful career.

* From the Common Destiny Alliance *(Realizing Our
Nation's Diversity as an Opportunity: Alternatives To
Sorting America's Children):*

The verdict is clear. Ability grouping is ineffective. It is
harmful to many students. It inhibits development of
interracial respect, understanding, and friendship. It
undermines democratic values and contributes to a
stratified society. There are effective and practical alternatives.
Ability grouping and tracking must end.

Charting a New Course

Changing social and economic conditions, along with greater awareness of tracking's drawbacks, present a variety of challenges to schools that set out to meet the needs of their students in the next century. In the absence of blueprints for inclusive schools, educators initially must invent new models and chart their reform course largely on their own. They must take the risk of creating schools where everyone learns at high levels.

Successful heterogeneous classrooms clearly require much more than simply regrouping students. Effective untracking demands simultaneous shifts in school organization, professional development, and teaching and learning activities — including assessment approaches and counseling responsibilities. Most of all, changes must produce more challenging learning opportunities for all students. They must "raise the floor and ceiling" for learning so that curriculum is not diluted and instruction is not geared "to the middle."

Different routes to common goals. In response to different conditions in communities, untracking schools follow many routes to shared goals. In some communities, untracking leads to adopting two-way bilingual schools, such as Milwaukee's Fratney Elementary School. In others, districts meet untracking goals by merging vocational and academic high school programs into a challenging technical curriculum — a strategy used by high schools in Cambridge, Massachusetts, and Forest Park, Georgia. In still others, untracking occurs as part of the opening of new magnet schools, the reorganization of a junior high into a middle school, or a district or school's affiliation with a network of reforming schools.

Whatever the route, untracking schools expect all their students to study side by side for higher level learning. Untracking educators share a triple commitment to:

* Eliminate the separation of groups of students;
* Extend academic and social support for high level learning to all students; and
* Ensure all students equal access to valued knowledge through multifaceted teaching strategies for high content curriculum.

These principles guide different schools as they seek improved achievement for more students as well as for the district as a whole.

W CHAPTER 3: HAT DO UNTRACKED SCHOOLS HAVE IN COMMON?

U ntracked schools are as diverse as the communities they serve. Yet, many share characteristics that highlight their dedication to providing equal access to knowledge and success for all in heterogeneous classrooms. Untracking is not an end in itself but a means to the end of improving learning for everyone.

High Expectations for All

W hile schools develop expected student outcomes in different ways, they are guided by two convictions. First, all children have the capacity to learn at high levels. Second, schools are the institutions responsible for developing this learning. For example, in the heterogeneously grouped classrooms at Wellesley Middle School in Massachusetts, a set of core beliefs about learning guide all educational decisions. These core beliefs are:

1. All students are capable of high achievement, not just our fastest and most confident learners.
2. Consistent effort leads to success.
3. You are not supposed to understand everything the first time around.
4. Mistakes help one to learn.

Wellesley's teachers have embraced these beliefs after discussing questions such as: Are the fastest answers always the smartest answers? Is competition necessary to motivate students and bring out the best in them? What kinds of schools and classrooms do we want for our own children?

Based on the beliefs that evolve from these discussions, Wellesley teachers reject ability grouping as a practice that undermines learning. As Principal John D'Auria says:

If tracking would help us accomplish our goals at this school, then we would use it. But we believe in producing active learners, critical thinkers, and risk takers,

and tracking our students by ability quite simply doesn't allow us to achieve our goals.

A rationale for untracking. Wellesley's core beliefs shape decisions about all aspects of school improvement, from staff development to teaching and curriculum reforms. In addition, the beliefs are a broader platform for explaining changes in student grouping, curriculum, and instruction to parents, school board members, and new teachers. D'Auria elaborates:

> Heterogeneous groupings will fail without the core beliefs. It is not enough to institute a policy change on any level without a basic understanding of what you want to do, why you want to do it, and what you need to accomplish your goals.

Teacher commitment drives change

Other principals agree that the success of untracking depends on teachers who honestly believe all students can learn. Teachers must be willing to engage in practices that help all students meet that expectation. As J.T. Crawford, principal of Crete-Monee Junior High School in Crete, Illinois, notes, "Everyone in the school has to be committed to the philosophy of high expectations, and you have to infuse every part of the school with that philosophy."

Edna Varner, principal of the Phoenix Middle School in Chattanooga, Tennessee, agrees. She explains:

> The key is that people really have to believe that a single track curriculum can work. There are good teachers who don't believe it because they don't know how to do it. They need tools to help them see what can happen for all kids.

Varner, like other principals, knows that when teachers have opportunities to see and try approaches that challenge students, they become believers. She adds:

> It's not about the good kids helping the slow kids. Teachers need to learn to plan for the things everyone has to struggle with. All kids struggle with discussing issues and improving their writing in response to questions like "What is justice and how do you achieve it?" The kids who have nothing to lose end up being risk-takers; they're unafraid of getting points deducted. When teachers see the dynamics of everyone working,

and no one is bored, then they become believers. The believing comes in our helping them know how.

Dennis Sparks, executive director of the National Staff Development Council, agrees. He notes that just as teachers need to communicate that all children can learn at high levels, teachers also need to believe that they and their colleagues can learn new, effective approaches for heterogeneous classrooms.

"The process of untracking requires teachers to be learners," he observes. "We have to examine our expectations for one another as part of the process of examining our expectations for kids."

Agreed-On Outcomes for All

In untracked schools, teachers in heterogeneous classes translate high expectations into clearly defined and expected outcomes for all students. For example, Pioneer Valley Regional School in Northfield, Massachusetts, has heterogeneously grouped students in grades 7-12 since 1985. The English Department identified the skills and knowledge students would master in ninth-tenth grade classes and in eleventh-twelfth grade classes.

Amy Mann, a teacher at Pioneer Valley, explains:

The skills list includes such expectations as, "Students will demonstrate critical and analytical reading and writing skills," [which] are specific regarding outcomes but don't confine teachers. Within the curriculum unit then, teachers can decide what kinds of assignments or projects will meet expected standards. Teachers also define grading criteria so that we can say, "This is the kind of work you have to do for an 'A,' or this kind of work reflects a 'B' standard."

Individual teachers develop learning activities that give students choices for mastering material. In Mann's heterogeneous classes, pairs of students choose from a list of paired authors — Ralph Waldo Emerson and Henry David Thoreau, Emily Dickinson and James Russell Lowell, Ezra Pound and T.S. Eliott, among others. Each student adopts the identity of one author. Mann then assigns each pair to exchange a series of letters on topics related to their lives, work, and community. This activity requires extensive reading, biographical research, and analysis of criticism of the authors' works.

Although Mann might modify assignments for students with disabilities to allow them more time or the use of different sources to complete their work, all students understand that they are expected to demonstrate skills and understanding of the subject.

Parallels with outcome-based education

The emphasis on outcomes in untracking schools parallels a variety of "outcomes-based" planning models, including the well-known "Outcomes-Driven Developmental Model" adopted by some schools as a key planning tool. As Brenda Lyons, director of secondary education and communications for Edmond, Oklahoma, Public Schools explains:

> The entire philosophy and teaching techniques associated with outcomes-based education are extensive and detailed. However, the main idea is that all students can succeed when given enough time. If a mastery learning model is followed with correctives given for students who do not master the material and enrichment provided for those who do, then students of all levels can be taught in the same classroom. As a result, tracking can be eliminated.

In some untracked schools, clear expected outcomes establish criteria not only for performance on specific assignments but also for graduation. In New York City's Central Park East Secondary School, for example, students must earn their diploma by compiling a series of portfolios that meet fourteen criteria in traditional subject areas as well as in autobiography, community service, ethics, practical skills, and physical challenge.

Ultimately, students must defend their work to a committee of educators and other adults from the community. While most students accomplish this required task over the course of their four-year high school program, some students complete the requirements in five years. Regardless of the time students need, a high level of effort and performance is consistent for all.

Making extra help available reduces the potential of some students being labeled "stupid" and strengthens the chances of everyone's success in heterogeneous classes.

Coaching To Help All Students

Believing that all students can learn at high levels and that they learn best in heterogeneous classes, untracked schools offer extra help in regular classes — with additional opportunities for coaching above and beyond these classes. Students achieving above "grade level" may receive coaching in creative writing or extension activities; others may benefit from tutoring on specific classroom or homework assignments.

Making extra help available reduces the potential of some students' being labeled "stupid" and strengthens the chances of everyone's success in heterogeneous classes. The various strategies untracked schools use to provide extra help often allow for some flexible ability grouping. In these cases, ability grouping is designed specifically to help students succeed in rigorous, heterogeneously grouped core courses.

The logistics of offering students extra help often involve re-structuring the school schedule. Many untracked schools have restructured their day into an eight- or even nine-period schedule to allow more time for coaching in particular areas. For example:

* At Castle High School near Honolulu, Hawaii, ninth- and tenth-grade students are grouped in heterogeneous classes for all core subjects. Those students who need extra help are slotted into homogeneous small groups during one of two "electives" periods or are enrolled in a double period in particular subjects. An extra period during the day also allows for "pre-teaching" to provide students who need it with a "jump start" in particular subject areas.

* At Willard Junior High School in Berkeley, California, students who score below the 30th percentile on state tests and who are eligible for Chapter 1 receive "pre-teaching." In these classes, students are introduced to curriculum units a week or two before the units are introduced in their heterogeneous classes.

In still other schools, the progress of individual students is monitored on a formal basis. For example:

* At the Prescott Middle School in Baton Rouge, Louisiana, students in danger of failing meet regularly with school counselors, teachers, and their parents to develop learning plans for strengthening study habits and building personal confidence.

Cross-Age Tutoring

A number of untracked schools develop extensive cross-age tutoring programs to support students in heterogeneous classes. Such an approach has been the cornerstone of a successful effort by the math department of Ponderosa High School in Parker, Colorado. Believing that all students should have access to a high quality curriculum, Ponderosa teacher Jim Reisinger instituted an innovative cross-age tutoring program to give students extra support. He explains:

In August 1991, I was given the two lowest track math courses. Unwilling to once again teach elementary- and junior-high-level math to sophomores, I began teaching them the same algebra course offered to the other students in the school. Acknowledging their inferior mathematical background (a result of earlier tracking), I used cross-age tutoring (CAT) for extra support.

The CAT program, consisting of older students acting in a mentor capacity to tutor younger students, has been extremely effective. There is no inferior status attached to receiving help from an older student as there is with peer tutoring. The older student is, in fact, a positive, motivating role model for the younger student. The CAT program also has the beneficial side effect of steering our most motivated students into a teaching career.

Reisinger explains in more detail how coordinating with other

(Continued, page 29.)

* At Valley Junior High School in Carlsbad, California, students experiencing academic difficulty are monitored closely. A Student Study Team coordinates tutors and extra support services.

Some schools make extra help available in as many settings as they have available to them. Thus, coaching for skills development may involve arranging for one-on-one tutoring with teachers or matching students with parent volunteers. For example:

* At Louis Armstrong Middle School in Queens, New York, any student who needs extra help is invited to come voluntarily to a before-school tutoring program where teachers are available to offer support. And while school officially begins at 8:40 a.m., the library is open for extra help starting at 8 a.m.

* At the Holyoke, Massachusetts, Magnet Middle School, teachers have formed a lunchtime "Math Club." While eating with their teachers, students discuss problems they might be having in their math classes. Teacher Marsha Bailey says, "Everyone has the same invitation, so there's no labeling or stigma. I tell students, 'The definition of a fine and admirable student is one who takes the initiative, who reaches out for what he or she needs and wants. That's what grown-ups do.'"

Finally, extra help for students also is extra help for teachers. For example, Montclair High School in New

Jersey has set up a writing center to support students enrolled in the school's challenging, heterogeneously grouped ninth-grade World Literature course. Two professional writers sharing the coordinator's job have trained 35 community volunteers. Volunteers comment on drafts of students' written work. The volunteers also join classes in the school's writing lab so that they can work with individual students on the spot.

Innovative Learning Strategies for All

Educators in schools with successful heterogeneous classrooms agree that regrouping students is likely to fail if teachers do not adopt new teaching and learning strategies. Multidimensional instruction for heterogeneous classes emphasizes thinking skills along with reading and math skills.

As classes become more heterogeneous — mixing academic performance, race, and gender — curriculum and instruction must challenge this more diverse group of learners. Teachers must know how to design complex, interesting learning activities that challenge students of all abilities.

Fred Newman and Gary Wehlage of the University of Wisconsin's Center on Organization and Restructuring of Schools have defined standards for authentic instruction that reflect teaching and learning in many

Algebra 1 classes and extra support has made higher mathematics available to students previously tracked at low levels:

We have four Algebra 1 classes, two of which are my pilot classes. The other two are taught by [another teacher] as a regular Algebra 1 class. We both started with about 60 students each (30 in each class). If a student had trouble in the regular class, he or she could transfer (if we agreed) to the pilot classes. Students who did well in the pilot class were transferred to the regular class. (About 20 students were switched.) All Algebra 1 classes are on the same page of Saxon's Algebra 1 text at the same time. They have the same tests too.

The only difference between the pilot and the regular classes is that my pilot class has a lot of help. In the classroom with me is a special education teacher and two special education adult aides. In addition, I have six student aids who are seniors (one junior) who work with the students, and I could use more. If a student is having a lot of trouble with the pilot, I have him or her assigned to me for another class period, and one of the student aides works with the student on his or her homework. (About five students are doubled up).

The experiment was a success. Students who had always been told that they were inferior to those on the higher track were suddenly proudly carrying the same book as

29

(Continued, page 30.)

every one of their peers. These students now not only have the academic background but also the confidence and self-esteem to meet the higher standards required for success in our society.

Based on this success, Reisinger has convinced Ponderosa's principal, Bill Larson, to hire a teacher aide to manage the cross-age tutors and provide a special tutoring center. Students cannot transfer from the class and can receive only credit grades of "A," "B," or "C." If a students is achieving below "C" level, he or she is assigned a class period for math tutoring, which may require a schedule change. Reisinger explains:

> In the tutoring sessions, the student is given individual help to complete the homework. It has been our experience that once a student is successful with the homework, success on tests follows naturally. It is amazing to watch a student who has had trouble with math in the past blossom and gain confidence to do math.

Ponderosa now enrolls all entering ninth-graders in algebra. Says Reisinger, "We're trying to make sure that all kids get the benefits of algebra when it counts — at the beginning of high school!" With talk about spreading the cross-age tutoring at Ponderosa to other subjects, Reisinger concludes, "Cross-age tutoring is a real power that has been forgotten in the structuring of our schools."

untracked schools. Five features of authentic instruction are:

1. Higher order thinking;
2. Depth of knowledge;
3. Connectedness to the world;
4. Substantive conversation; and
5. Social support for student achievement.

In traditional schools, these characteristics often are found only in high level classes. Increasingly, untracked schools are weaving authentic instruction into teaching and learning activities in heterogeneous classes through Socratic seminars, cooperative learning, complex instruction, thematic curricula, including attention to multicultural perspectives, and high level learning for special groups.

Socratic seminars

Socratic seminars are a learning technique to stimulate inquiry and force students to think critically, apply knowledge and skills to new situations, articulate opinions, listen, make decisions, and resolve conflicts.

At the Chattanooga School for the Arts and Sciences in Tennessee, inquiry for understanding is built into the program of every student in grades 1-12. In weekly, 80-minute Socratic seminars, heterogeneous groups of students reflect on and discuss specific texts assigned to all students in each grade. Every teacher is assigned to one seminar group, so learning groups are small. All students participate in discussions that emphasize learning for understanding.

Socratic seminars also are a fundamental part of instruction at Chattanooga's five Paideia schools. Teachers meet regularly to discuss appropriate questions that will probe students' opinions and deepen their understanding of ideas in the assigned reading. Each semester, the seminar committees select readings or other works of art submitted by faculty, students, and parents.

Discussion sources. Seminar readings may come from books or other publications, such as seventh-grade readings at CSAS of "Storm Over the Amazon," an essay by Harvard entomologist Edward O. Wilson, or Eugene Linder's September 23, 1991, *Time* cover story, "Lost Tribes, Lost Knowledge." However, readings are never from a textbook and are not always entire books, reflecting Paideia's belief that students can develop in-depth understanding from fragments of valuable works. One exception is an early fall seminar devoted to discussion of one required book from the summer reading list —*Tuck Everlasting,* by Natalie Babbitt, for sixth-graders and *The Outsiders,* by S. E. Hinton, for seventh- and eighth-graders. Seminar periods also may be used to discuss special topics, such as a senior student-led discussion on the presidential election.

At another Paideia school, Chattanooga's Phoenix Middle School, Principal Edna Varner says the seminars are her school's most successful experience with heterogeneous grouping:

> The hardest part of "seminaring" is coming up with good questions. Teachers have to ask questions that do not have a right or wrong answer but require going to the text to form an opinion and going back to the text for supporting arguments. The kids really start thinking. They learn that when they express learned opinions based on knowledge or research, these are the ones that make the most compelling arguments. They begin to learn how important those supporting details are. They learn about the importance of reading widely.

Phoenix Middle School schedules all seminars in the morning, usually for 45 rather than 80 minutes "for the teachers' comfort level." "At first, teachers are most nervous about keeping the kids talking," Varner explains. However, when such stimulating readings as the short story "The Lady or the Tiger?" are the basis for discussion, "kids are talking for the first time, and they don't want to stop. What they find in the seminar is that they understand concepts of freedom, grief, guilt, the dynamics of friendship, and about wanting something but not knowing how to get it."

Schools do not have to be identified as Paideia schools to employ more dialogue and discussion in multiability classes. Some untracked schools adopt a packaged curriculum, such as the Philosophy for Children or the Junior Great Books Program. Others infuse conversation and inquiry into their own teacher-designed activities. In both cases, the divergent thinking that characterizes heterogeneous classrooms is a particular asset to learning and in-depth understanding about topics such as "What is success?" or "What constitutes power?"

Cooperative learning

The change from traditional teacher-centered instruction to cooperative learning is the most well-known difference in untracked schools. What does such a shift look like?

* Student "teams," usually of four students, are heterogeneously grouped so that one "high," two "average," and one "low" ability student work together. Team member composition changes every six to nine weeks so students get used to working with different team members.

* Students receive explicit instruction in social skills that emphasizes cooperation and teamwork.

* Improved learning for all is the goal. While students are held accountable for their own learning, they also take responsibility for helping one another.

* Students clearly understand the objectives of the work they are assigned. If students complete the activities early, they are directed to additional independent activities of their choice.

* Instruction moves from a teacher-based focus to a partner- or group-based focus on independent learning and direct instruction. Thus, cooperative learning does not completely replace direct instruction, but it reinforces and enhances teacher-transmitted knowledge.

* Rewards for both individual student effort and for teams are built into learning.

A number of well-researched cooperative learning approaches fit these characteristics, and many are widely used in untracking schools. Teachers report that cooperative learning is especially effective for students who have experienced little success in traditionally organized classes.

Models such as Cooperative Integrated Reading and Composition, Learning Together, Group Investigation, Jigsaw, Team-Games-Tournament, Student Teams-Achievement Division, and Team-Assisted Individualization offer teachers a repertoire of strategies to accommodate wide-ranging differences in skill and achievement levels in mixed-ability classrooms. Several of these approaches allow teachers to mix students heterogeneously or homogeneously.

Built-in success. These approaches have a positive impact on student achievement, attitudes toward school, and peer relations. In fact, success is built into the design of cooperative learning. As Robert Stevens of Johns Hopkins University explains, "The whole system is designed around mastery. If you do everything you're supposed to do, there's no need for failure. You should have every kid succeed. Everyone can be a winner."

Cooperative learning alone does not transform heterogeneous classes into high performance classes. For greatest effect, teachers must be aware of student interaction problems that may impede learning, especially those that arise when students of different social status are enrolled in heterogeneous classes.

Complex instruction

Stanford University researchers Elizabeth Cohen, Beatriz Arias, and others have focused on improving the achievement of children who often are assigned limited social status — and lower expectations — in their classrooms. Ethnicity, language accent, perceived academic or reading ability, popularity, or length of time in the United States are some factors that might lead to lower social status for a child. Cohen and Aris' approach, called complex instruction, offers specific techniques to:

* Create changes in classroom organization and management.

* Introduce a multiple-ability curriculum.

* Strengthen teacher-student interventions to reduce status differences among students.
* Support teaching staff to improve achievement for all children.

In complex instruction, students work in small, heterogeneous groups where they must talk with and help one another complete problem-solving tasks at different learning centers. While reading, writing, and computation are embedded in each assignment, tasks themselves focus on interesting, demanding concepts. Each task also requires students to use different learning materials and intelligences — an approach that takes into account students' varied learning styles. The following examples illustrate this practice.

Classes at Davidson Middle School in San Rafael, California, use complex instruction techniques. Immigrant students from a variety of countries work together in a language arts-social studies curriculum to develop basic skills, while exploring topics in anthropology, economics, and history. For example:

* Based on a reading of the story, "Boy of the Painted Cave," students explore imaginary cultures created by student teams. They describe these cultures with visual clues about geography, cuisine, division of labor, tools, weapons, and belief systems. Once each group has developed its "culture," others examine the "discovered" cave paintings, hypothesizing about that culture's development in response to given environmental conditions.
* After reading stories aloud as a class, students work in small groups to answer questions, analyzing character and plot. Based on one reading, *Geronimo: His Own Story*, individual students design a storyboard to illustrate the significant events of a life, incorporating visual icons into their descriptions.

The richness of these assignments clearly accommodates diverse learners. "Tasks should be open-ended so that precocious students can carry them further, while less mature students can complete the tasks on a simpler level," emphasizes researcher Cohen.

Setting the ground rules. Teachers explicitly instruct students in how to learn and work in groups, and they make two distinct rules: "You have the right to ask anyone else at your learning center for help," and "You have the duty to assist anyone who asks for help." These rules maximize student involvement and limit classroom management problems. Rotating students' assigned roles, including the role of "facilitator," promotes greater student interaction and results in achievement gains.

Complex instruction also calls on teachers to explain two specific "status treatments" or explicit teachings about students working in small groups. First, teachers communicate that successfully completing assigned tasks requires many different skills, not just reading and writing. They announce to the class that no one person will be good at everything, but everyone will be good at something. Teachers observe low-status students for demonstrations of competence at a particular intellectual ability necessary to the assignment. The teacher will then explain what the student did and why this specific skill is valuable in the adult world. These techniques equalize and increase student interaction in diverse classrooms, which helps teachers bring about significant achievement gains for low-status students.

Learning About New Teaching Strategies

Teachers in untracking schools learn about cooperative learning and complex instruction in a variety of ways. Milwaukee's Parkman Middle School has created the role of "teacher facilitator" for one faculty member who works directly with teachers in their classrooms to demonstrate cooperative learning activities and peer coaching. More frequently, schools invite teachers to attend multisession training workshops, then set up times for them to get together and exchange successes and failures.

Many educators believe that staff development in cooperative learning is most effective when implemented with specific curriculum changes. For example, the California-based Teachers' Curriculum Institute integrates staff development with rich examples of activities and materials for a multidimensional secondary school curriculum in history and social studies. Likewise, the Massachusetts-based Educators for Social Responsibility incorporates cooperative learning activities into an interdisciplinary curriculum that combines mathematics and social studies learning. Activities engage heterogeneously grouped students in applying information from the 1990 census to mathematical problem solving.

Interested educators can keep abreast of developments in the cooperative learning field through *Cooperative Learning* magazine, which collects current information about theory, research, curricula, and instruction as well as concrete suggestions for classroom activities and staff development. The magazine's sponsoring organization, the International Association for the Study of Cooperation in Education, also can steer untracking schools to many resources. The association can be reached at 136 Liberty St., Santa Cruz, CA 95060; (408) 429-6550.

Thematic curriculum

To foster in-depth learning for all students, many untracking schools are refocusing their curricula away from "coverage" of a wide range of material into a single theme. Some schools organize learning around themes within a single discipline. Others work to incorporate several subject areas into one theme. Either way, themes allow students to explore many aspects of one topic.

The point of a thematic curriculum is to offer students of various abilities and learning styles increased learning opportunities. At Pioneer Valley Regional School in Northfield, Massachusetts, for example, secondary teacher Karen Morgan uses a single "anchor book" or principle text as a foundation for teaching themes as varied as "Native Americans," "Censorship and Banned Books," or "Growing Old." The anchor books give students a framework for discussing plot, character, and theme.

Students then select additional novels that Morgan pulls together from the school library, her personal collection, and ten-cent finds from yard sales and flea markets. Explains Morgan, "With this system, I have to be on top of what every student is reading. If someone's bored, I jump in. Whatever their level, the kids are never allowed to stop reading."

Morgan's trust in her students' reading choices has developed with experience. At first, she distributed books to students according to her perceptions of their abilities. But that changed. She explains:

Students knew exactly what I was doing. I found I'd made a mistake thinking I could restrict their reading. So the next year, I put all the books on the table and let the kids choose. What happens is that they make their choices according to their interest in the story. Some very good readers choose "easy" books, but that's all right because they still have to think about the ideas in the story, and they still get pleasure from the literature. And some kids you'd never expect choose the harder books. One of my poorer readers chose to read Conrad Richter's **Light in the Forest**. It took him all semester, and at the end he said it was the "most awesome" book he'd ever read. I never would have assigned that book to him.

All the pieces fit together. In Pioneer Valley classes, all language arts activities relate to the reading theme. Practice using prepositional phrases and new vocabulary evolves from the novels students select. Likewise, writing assignments reinforce reading to stimulate writing original work or researching and writing in social sciences. Students also might write a letter to a guest speaker about the impact of the theme on their lives. Another teacher, Amy Mann, explains:

> Thematic curriculum works beautifully in a heterogeneous classroom because it allows for choice and mandates working together for maximum comprehension....A thematic approach to teaching literature...stimulates a heterogeneous group to do the real analytical work we crave from our literature students because inherent in this approach is choice. Many interesting and diverse pieces of literature can be offered to students. Not everyone has to read the same thing, as long as the piece has to do with the theme.

> Not only does reading different material create choices for students, but it also mandates that students learn to see connections and patterns in literature. Such learning, I believe, is the thematic approach's most important value.

Diversity enriches the theme. Educators who have developed thematic curricula emphasize using themes as a springboard for active learning and long-term projects. For example, Judy Pace, a researcher who worked on the development of the interdisciplinary curriculum "Immigration 1850" at Harvard University's Project Zero, explains that a thematic curriculum should engage students in applying all kinds of intelligences and in using different kinds of strengths through multidimensional projects.

"In project work, it's beneficial to have a group of students who bring a variety of intelligences to the tasks. Skills are embedded in a rich context, and diversity becomes a positive asset in understanding that context," Pace said.

Through the "Immigration 1850" curriculum software, for example, students refer to recorded historical data to compile graphs or charts of employment opportunities in the 1850s, create three-dimensional models of 19th century housing, and compare 1850 prices and wages with those of the 1990s. They may read articles from the immigrant community newspaper to gain a perspective on westward expansion and social conditions preceding the Civil War. Or, they may write letters "home," present skits or plays for other classmates, interview contemporary immigrants or family members about their immigration experiences, or create a collection of artifacts to hand down to subsequent generations of their "family."

Some teachers in untracking schools may opt to use a packaged curriculum such as "Immigration 1850." Others develop their own curricula that reflect their surroundings. For example, at Islander Middle School in Mercer Island, Washington, teachers have developed high level learning around grade-specific themes of "Ships" and "The Renaissance" for the sixth grade, and "The Pacific Northwest" for the seventh. "Democracy" is one of the themes for eighth-graders, who learn about their rights and responsibilities as citizens.

Themes present many opportunities for nontraditional learning activities such as field trips, guest speakers, art projects, pen pals, and oral histories. Teachers also can incorporate different multicultural perspectives into their instruction.

A link to the real world. In occupational programs, themes are a way to merge academic and technical arts curricula. For example, at the Rindge and Latin High School in Cambridge, Massachusetts, curriculum coordinator Adria Steinberg and a team of technical arts teachers have fashioned a ninth-grade curriculum organized around an in-depth study of their 100,000-person, multiethnic city. Students examine their city's architecture, design plan, services, people, neighborhoods, industries, and trades. Projects expose students to the occupational studies offered at their school while allowing them to continue taking academic subjects.

Multicultural curriculum

In Montclair, New Jersey, a racially diverse community near Newark, English teachers had long been dismayed that their high school's system of allowing students to choose their ninth-grade  courses only resegregated students by race. Many African American students would choose courses based on their perceived low ability or because they knew their friends were in certain classes, which were usually not the advanced courses.

As Bernadette Anand, chairperson of the school's English department, recalls:

> Black students were just not finding their way into our [challenging, high level] 1A courses. All of us in the English department decided we should get more minority students into the 1A program, but we also knew that students would not sit in classes where they did not see their faces reflected in the curriculum. We had to change what it was we taught if we were going to succeed.

Over several years of meeting with parents, students, and teachers to think, plan, and pilot new curricula, the department devised a five-credit, year-long core course for all ninth-graders on "World Cultures and Literature." Class membership is intentionally balanced by race, gender, and academic performance, bringing a richness of perspectives to discussions.

The premise of the course is that high quality literature is best appreciated from multiple perspectives, including those presented in the readings and students' reactions to them. During the first month of the school year, students discuss attitudes and assumptions reflected in a wide range of poetry and folklore, the drama **Twelve Angry Men**, and John Steinbeck's novel, **Of Mice and Men**. Through close reading of texts, journal writing, discussion of vocabulary and language, simulations, and field trips, students begin to apply concepts, look for missing perspectives, tease out unspoken assumptions, and analyze characters from different points of view.

Beyond book reports. Over the course of the year, students study texts from a wide range of cultures, including Native American, Middle Eastern, Western European, African, Greek, Roman, Japanese, and Chinese literature. Literary discussions consider creation myths and proverbs reflecting common themes from various cultures. Each unit involves not only reading and writing but classroom activities such as cooperative problem solving, filmstrips, and music. Students work collaboratively and individually on extension projects — map- or model-making, oral presentations or book talks, or investigation of games or art forms that reflect themes found in literature and life. By the end of the year, students have created their own portfolios of what they have learned.

Extensive staff development in lesson design, cooperative learning, and the teacher's role in a heterogeneous setting have helped prepare teachers for implementing the world cultures course.

During the last weeks of summer vacation, teachers in the department held a three-day meeting with Dennie Palmer Wolfe of the Harvard Graduate School of Education to discuss and develop alternative means of assessing students' work. In addition, support from writing coaches at the high school-based writing center, a class size of 22, and a series of parent awareness sessions at the eighth-grade level all focus on ensuring success for every student in this challenging setting.

Tapping into social and personal concerns. Elsewhere in New Jersey, Kay Goerss, former teacher supervisor of West Windsor-Plainsboro Middle School, reports that the school's curriculum increasingly connects student learning to the wider world. West Windsor-Plainsboro already has developed an interdisciplinary curriculum for its heterogeneously grouped seventh-graders.

Students first choose a set of social issues they want to study in-depth. Working in cooperative teams, students use skills from all subject areas to produce detailed magazines on each topic. Goerss explains:

> The magazines pull all the subject areas together. Students have to use math skills to produce charts, tables, and graphs to illustrate their topic. They use research in social studies and science to gather and organize information, and their literature selections — the school uses reading workshops, writing-across-the-curriculum, and whole language approaches — include readings on biracial families and family interaction, economics, the environment, and problems of segregation and integration. [The experience is] different from year to year since it all grows from the kids deciding what social concerns they're going to look at.

At West Windsor-Plainsboro, week-long schoolwide projects also promote interdisciplinary social activities that touch on all parts of the school's curriculum. For example, just prior to the winter holidays, a week-long focus on cultural diversity extends to physical education classes where students learn games from around the world.

High level learning for special groups

When differences between low- and high-achieving students are dramatic, heterogeneous grouping may seem like an insurmountable challenge. Before all students can succeed in a high level curriculum, schools may need to invest some extra time and resources into helping those furthest behind grade level.

Even when untracking schools decide that some students — such as immigrant or Chapter 1 students — need instruction in special groups, they ensure that teaching and learning will be challenging and nurturing. Moreover, instruction in these special groupings has the ultimate goal of bringing students into high level heterogeneous classes.

> *Teachers reject instruction that focuses on parts of a subject at the expense of the whole, memorization of facts apart from their context, and a narrow emphasis on basic skills to the exclusion of inherently challenging assignments.*

Higher order thinking activities are emphasized as the context for strengthening skills. Teachers reject instruction that focuses on parts of a subject at the expense of the whole, memorization of facts apart from their context, and a narrow emphasis on basic skills to the exclusion of inherently challenging assignments. Instead, teachers choose approaches that add meaning, coherence, and depth to their students' learning. These approaches orient students to whole concepts prior to breaking the larger learning focus into parts. Learning situations relate directly to students' interests and real life.

Intensive writing for ESL students. Rather than memorizing vocabulary lists or spending most of their time working on oral communication, students in Mary Fipp's transitional English classroom at Muirlands Middle School in the San Diego City School District spend their double language arts period reading whole texts and writing intensively. English is the second language for these sixth-graders, who generally have scored two or more grades below grade level in reading comprehension.

Fipp notes, "Books selected for the program, **The Whipping Boy, In the Year of the Boar,** and **Jackie Robinson,** for example, incorporate a vocabulary that is manageable, yet include themes that are universal, intriguing, and contemporary." Students keep journals and literature logs on a regular basis. Writing assignments are interwoven with their reading.

By mid-year, students come to see themselves as "writers," and many complain when a special event at the school interrupts their writing time. During one year, over 60 percent of the students made gains of two or more years in reading comprehension none made less than a one-year gain. And all students were better prepared for their challenging seventh-grade classes.

Success with Chapter 1 students. For Chapter 1 classes, HOTS, the Higher Order Thinking Skills program developed by Stanley Pogrow at the University of Arizona's College of Education, presumes that some students are academically "at risk" because they have not learned reflective thinking skills. Designed as a "gifted approach for at-risk learners," the HOTS curriculum is a general thinking program that helps students learn to deal with several concepts simultaneously, engage in dialogue about ideas, think in terms of general principles, and pursue ideas to their logical conclusions.

HOTS teachers use carefully worded questions to probe students about how they reached particular conclusions and why their answers are correct or incorrect. Following a theory of "controlled floundering," teachers encourage students to slow down and think carefully rather than to guess wildly at quick answers.

Socratic conversations take place about problems posed through a variety of computer games such as "Murder by the Dozen" or "Where in the World Is Carmen San Diego?" In these conversations, teachers critique students' responses in a constructive, nurturing way, using phrases such as, "What makes you think that?" or "What do you think this character means when he says this?"

In turn, students have to make decisions based on gathered evidence and predicted consequences. They learn that:

✱ Thoughtful answers require more than one word;

✱ Problems often generate more than one right answer;

✱ Specific examples are different from general principles;

✱ You can learn something from wrong answers; and

✱ Persistence leads to improvement.

On "Invite a Friend Day," HOTS students share these insights with classmates they select from outside their HOTS immediate classroom. Follow-up studies of HOTS suggest that after two years of the program, low-performing students do not need additional remedial services, and many attain "honor roll" status in their school.

Pumping Minority Students into Algebra

Students who take algebra by the end of middle school or beginning of high school have greater access to higher mathematics courses and are better prepared to do well on college entrance examinations. However, tracking and ability grouping in math typically exclude many poor and minority students from this critical "gatekeeping" course.

To remedy this pattern, the College Board established the Equity 2000 program in 1990. As participants in this project, six urban school districts pledged to enroll increasing numbers of eighth- and ninth-graders in algebra and to provide them with needed support to succeed in the course.

The project is located in six sites, each with a significant minority and disadvantaged population: Fort Worth, Texas; Milwaukee, Wisconsin; Nashville, Tennessee; Prince George's County, Maryland; Providence, Rhode Island; and San Jose, California.

According to the College Board, between 60 to 97 percent of all ninth-graders now are taking algebra or a more advanced mathematics course, compared to 31 to 69 percent three years ago. Just as important, more students are passing these courses. For example, in the Fort Worth Independent School District, enrollment in algebra has jumped by a third, and the number passing algebra has increased 14.5 percent.

By 1993-94, nearly 500,000 K-12 students in more than 700 schools across the country were participating in the program.

Equity 2000's success can be attributed to several key factors. Teachers in all six districts participated in staff development using standards developed by the National Council of Teachers of Mathematics. Districts also supported student learning through coaching strategies such as Saturday academies and tutoring.

For more information on Equity 2000, contact The College Board, 45 Columbus Ave., New York, NY 10023-6992; (212) 713-8268.

Open to everyone. In many elementary and middle schools, HOTS is a Chapter 1 pull-out program featuring small classes in separate settings. In addition, some untracking schools offer HOTS in heterogeneous classes. For example, the Prescott Middle School in Baton Rouge, Louisiana, makes HOTS available as an elective course in thinking skills. Principal Anna Bernard explains:

The first year, our HOTS lab was the program of choice for students who failed any one of three parts on our state-mandated exam. It was a terrific success. We were impressed! When we looked at the program, we saw there was no need to limit it to a few students. We applied for a special grant, and the second year we were able to double the class, and now we offer it to anyone who wants to take it.

Prescott's HOTS lab has 17 computers, which allows at least that number of students to work with a teacher and aide each period of the seven-period day. Bernard rejects the notion that only a few selected students should benefit from a new program. "If it's here, it's open to everyone," she says.

Prescott Middle School has replaced its remedial classes with a single, multidimensional curriculum for all students, meaning HOTS classes are heterogeneously grouped. Bernard explains:

> We have "honor roll kids" and kids with behavioral problems all in the same class, and you cannot pick these kids out. It's a different learning atmosphere. In HOTS, there's a clean slate. There's no past garbage. Everyone starts off equal. After a week or so, they learn how to cooperate. The teacher did not have to send one child to the office from the HOTS class the whole year.

Bernard and her teachers also credit HOTS with positively changing students' attitudes. Bernard notes:

> HOTS has really improved student attitudes toward learning. You know, if you go into many traditional classrooms, kids are asked to raise their hands and speak out. But if children have a long record of failure, they are hesitant to risk. HOTS encourages kids to take chances, to make guesses. You can walk into a HOTS class, and the kids want to tell you what they predict might happen if they do one thing or another. They learn to learn from their wrong guesses, and they get support for taking risks.

The best for all. Clearly, untracking schools adopt many learning approaches, and no one strategy meets all situations. However, untracking efforts share a commitment to developing teachers' skills for working with students in heterogeneous classrooms at levels typically reserved for "top-track" students. In setting high standards for all students, untracking teachers weave together multiple instructional threads to make their multiability classes just as challenging — if not more challenging — as traditional "advanced" groups.

"We have 'honor roll kids' and kids with behavioral problems all in the same class, and you cannot pick these kids out. It's a different learning atmosphere."

Structures and Routines Support Inclusive Learning

Untracking schools value student effort over achievement and cooperation over competition. Their structures and routines reflect this emphasis.

Interdisciplinary teams

Many untracking schools begin using teams when they change over to heterogeneous grouping. Teams typically include core curriculum teachers, special education teachers, and other specialists who pair with "regular" teachers in core subject classrooms. They collaborate to plan, organize, and implement instruction for their students who are divided into smaller clusters within a school.

Common planning time. Team teachers meet regularly, ideally at least several times a week, in a common planning period. Working cooperatively, they discuss the learning needs of specific students. By setting common high expectations, norms, and rules, teachers send a consistent message to students about discipline, homework, and accountability. Teachers who work together rather than "solo" also are more likely to discuss and seek solutions to problems related to basic school structures, including tracking.

On their own, teaming and common planning time do not guarantee successful heterogeneous grouping. Unless educators are sensitive to grouping issues, teams may even become tracks themselves, with the labels "gifted" or "basic." However, when heterogeneously grouped teams vary by subject, respond to individual student needs, and reflect the diversity of student demographics, they can become viable alternatives to tracking. Thus, within one large school, one heterogeneously grouped team might offer two-way bilingual learning while another might organize activities around multidimensional intelligence theories. Although somewhat different in focus, each team would seek to meet common learning goals.

Nongraded alternatives. In some untracked schools, teams are organized around nongraded grouping arrangements. Robert Anderson, coauthor of *The Nongraded Elementary School*, points out that authentic nongraded schools or teams should:

* Replace grades with titles that reflect the concept of continuous progress, such as "primary unit."
* Include at least two heterogeneous age cohorts in all groupings.
* Use temporary instructional groupings that can be dissolved and reconstituted as needed.

"We now know that the most natural learning environment for children calls for heterogeneous multiage groupings, within which all sorts of homogeneous and heterogeneous subgroupings can be created as needed," he adds.

The Clara Barton Open School in Minneapolis, Minnesota, and the Bennett Park Public Montessori School in Buffalo, New York, have embraced multiability grouping in multiage, nongraded primary and middle-level classrooms. Student groupings resemble family patterns, with students of different ages interacting with one another.

Scheduling changes

Flexible school schedules — especially in middle and high schools — benefit heterogeneous grouping and the classroom changes that support it. For example, in-depth project learning, hands-on science activities, and Socratic seminars often require blocks of time that extend beyond the traditional 50-minute period. Moreover, teachers' may need to set aside extra time for coaching students in specific skills. If teams are responsible for scheduling, teachers have the flexibility and time to address these needs.

Expanding learning opportunities

Believing that all school activities are learning opportunities, many untracked schools include all interested students in activities that traditionally were open only to the most confident learners. Some schools, especially in the middle grades, implement "no cut" policies for cheerleading and intermural sports teams. All interested students, including those with physical disabilities, are allowed to participate.

For example, Jericho, New York, Middle School ensures that all interested students receive a speaking part in dramatic productions, either by putting on multiple performances or by writing in additional speaking parts to accommodate them. In such ways, effort, commitment, and interest, rather than native ability, are rewarded.

Expanding recognition of effort and achievement

Educators who take multiple intelligence theories seriously devise ways for their students to apply and develop their intelligence. This commitment usually involves changing to assessment strategies where students demonstrate what they have learned and are able to do. By substituting exhibitions and demonstrations for purely paper-and-pencil tests, schools communicate that applying learning in visual, musical, interpersonal, and intrapersonal ways is valuable in the real world. Minneapolis' Clara Barton Open School also asks students to assess their own effort and learning outcomes so that they begin to internalize standards of high performance.

In line with such performance-based assessment strategies, many untracked schools have abandoned "weighted" grades or "quality points" in student assessment. Instead, they use classroom rubrics that describe specifically what constitutes proficiency in a discipline and what is required from students on particular assignments. These schools also build in routines to ensure all students are recognized for their efforts. For example, students at Crete-Monee Junior High in Illinois can sign an academic improvement contract pledging to bring up grades in two subjects without letting others slip. Fulfillment of the contract wins them a place on the honor roll.

> *"Smart is not something you are. Smart is something you get."*

At the core of all these changes is the belief, expressed by Jeffrey Howard, president of the Efficacy Institute in Lexington, Massachusetts, that "Smart is not something you are. Smart is something you get." Pioneering educators aspire to create communities of learners in which all students have as many opportunities as possible to develop their intelligence and abilities — in academic classes, co-curricular activities, and community service. In these schools, early and late bloomers alike have the opportunity to excel.

Principal Sandra Caldwell of the Middle School of the Kennebunks in Maine, sums up this philosophy: "In our school, every student can be smart every single day."

Counseling All Students for Success

M any students — especially in high poverty school districts or in districts with large, comprehensive high schools — often do not connect their school courses with future opportunities. Some have limited or no access to information that can help them make future-oriented decisions. Others might get steered into dead-end tracks by well-meaning counselors used to sorting students into differentiated programs "for their own good."

In untracked schools, a counselor's responsibility shifts from gatekeeping to expanding students' opportunities. Counselors do not just provide information about the consequences of course choices and placements. Instead, they actively build on students' own aspirations and talents to help them develop the confidence, motivation, and decision-making skills needed in accelerated courses.

Supporting success in heterogeneous groups

The counseling staff at Massachusetts' Pioneer Valley Regional School took deliberate steps to support student success in heterogeneous groups, communicate high expectations, and stimulate students to take advantage of future opportunities. After eight years of working with mostly heterogeneously grouped students through 12th grade, counselor Dona Cadwell looks back on "the old days":

> Being responsible for placing students in different levels in grades seven through nine felt extremely uncomfortable. It was like playing God with so many unknowns, unopened minds, unexplored options, and a lack of knowledge of the world. The kids usually trusted us. Parents wanted the best, even if students were not recommended for the high levels, and students would be made to feel inferior if they couldn't handle the work in the particular group. Often the difference in work was amount rather than difficulty. The very act of labeling was repulsive.

In contrast, counseling in an untracked setting honors students' ambitions and future plans. "Now we work with students to help them make decisions regarding different math and science courses," Cadwell says. "Still, many students choose more difficult courses and feel confident or ready to take a risk. Most succeed."

Since Pioneer Valley began helping students learn about and expand their future opportunities, the school's rate of students going on to college has increased dramatically. Cadwell advises other schools interested in following Pioneer Valley's lead to:

✳ Expect that every student eventually will go on to postsecondary education. Provide all students with information to help them identify people with similar skills and interests who have gone to college and ended up in interesting occupations.

✳ Repeat college admissions requirements in every grade. Beginning in the middle grades, ask questions that communicate the expectation that your students will consider college, such as "Which language did you choose?" or "Are you ready for algebra now?"

✳ Tell students about how particular graduates' high school experiences contributed to their postsecondary success: "Most of our students who have gone on to college tell me how much they use computers..."

✳ Bring in resource people who are able to inspire and relay information about occupations and their education requirements.

✳ Work with teachers on career-investigation projects.

✳ Share newspaper clippings about successful people and how they reached their goals.

✳ Publicize college video screenings or lend videos to students to take home.

✳ Run parent workshops to let them know about options and opportunities for their children.

Vital information, vital choices. Clearly, access to guidance resources allows students to make informed choices about their studies. Middle grades counselors should provide information and assistance to all students about high school courses and their requirements, with a goal of increasing the numbers of students enrolling in college preparatory courses. Administrators need to support counselors by making educational guidance a priority. They also can monitor and recognize schools with increased rates of students going on to college — keeping a close eye on the progress of poor, African American, and Latino students.

In its publication ***Keeping the Options Open***, The College Board emphasizes that counselors must work with students to enhance their academic performance and help them make choices that will expand their opportunities. The report's major recommendations urge schools as a whole to motivate students academically by:

* Establishing a broad-based process in each local school district for determining the particular guidance and counseling needs of the students within each school and for planning how best to meet those needs.

* Developing a program under the leadership of each school principal that emphasizes the importance of the guidance counselor as a monitor and promoter of student potential as well as a coordinator of the school's guidance plan.

* Mounting programs to inform and involve parents and other influential family members in the planning, decision-making, and learning activities of the student.

* Providing a program of guidance and counseling during the early and middle years of schooling, especially for students who traditionally have not been well-served by the schools.

As the role of the guidance counselor evolves from providing services to coordinating services, he or she becomes a critical part of the academic team, rather than an adjunct to it.

Supporting learning in challenging courses

In the San Diego County Public Schools, middle and high school counselors are shifting away from sorting students by following a program called AVID, Achieving Via Individual Determination. Begun by counselor Mary Catherine Swanson as an effort to boost the representation of African American and Latino students in high level courses, AVID places students typically tracked into lower academic levels in the most rigorous courses offered by their school.

However, the district does not throw these students into a fast-moving stream of advanced courses. A comprehensive system of support services is available to help students succeed in the new settings. These services include motivational activities, tutoring, and workshops on study skills, note-taking, and asking questions. Students learn to use binders and record-keeping forms to document their experiences and to recount difficulties with particular academic assignments or projects.

Students helping students. In addition, counselors work with teachers to organize students into study groups where they help each other clarify questions about their assignments and learn how to ask for specific help. College tutors, many of whom are AVID graduates, facilitate the student groups. Tutors serve as role models, coaches, and motivators for students.

"We intentionally cultivate students' ability to work together in groups," says AVID teacher Kathy Deering. "We want our students to graduate not only eligible for and enrolled in — but also to be successful in — postsecondary education." The goal of keeping students in college once they get there is especially meaningful in California, where the average job now requires 13.6 years of education.

At each AVID school, school counselors are active participants on the academic support team. To make the program work, they must schedule students into college preparatory courses, help prepare students for college entry tests, arrange for field trips to colleges, and assist in college and financial aid application processes. After experiencing years of remedial curricula and low expectations, many students entering the AVID program can scarcely imagine academic success. Counselors must work closely with these students to keep their motivation alive.

AVID's results demonstrate how combining access to meaningful knowledge with intensive, group-centered support, tutoring, and motivational activities makes heterogeneous grouping successful. From 1986 to 1990, the dropout rate in AVID schools declined by 37 percent; at the same time, 98.8 percent of AVID graduates have enrolled in college. In 1991, senior classes at AVID sites completed four-year college entry requirements at a rate 140 percent higher than the statewide rate.

Expanding future opportunities for students

Many students leave the eighth grade with little information about how their decisions about ninth-grade courses will influence later learning opportunities. Many students enroll in course sequences that school staff choose for them, rather than in an academic program based on their own interests and aspirations. Still others miss out on critical "gatekeeping" or prerequisite courses in ninth grade, so they fall behind early in high school. Once behind, it is difficult to transfer into more attractive sequences later.

According to the College Entrance Examination Board, vital postsecondary counseling resources are not equally distributed among students. For example, middle school students from poor, rural, and urban families are less likely than their more advantaged peers to get appropriate guidance in selecting high school courses. The less access to counseling students have, the more likely they are to be placed in curricular tracks with fewer academic courses.

Strengthening Planning Skills

At Crete-Monee Junior High School in Crete, Illinois, counselors understand that a smooth transition between the eighth and ninth grade, especially when it means moving from one new school into another, depends on students' knowledge of high school courses and their future plans. Students also need to understand how specific courses are prerequisites for future educational and career opportunities.

Crete-Monee's innovative counseling program helps students develop a written four-year plan to match their high school careers with their personal aspirations. Once students are aware of the connection between courses and their future plans, they see the rationale for enrolling in more difficult courses and are less likely to let counselors or others choose their high school classes for them.

Planning starts early. Seventh-graders at Crete-Monee begin to design their high school plan as part of a classroom-based course, using a curriculum the district's counseling staff has adopted. The curriculum, "Pathways to Success: Individualized Educational and Career Plan (ICEP)," helps students assess their strengths, weaknesses, values, interests, and abilities. Through a series of hands-on activities, students learn about their interests and acquire information about the occupations and postsecondary educational opportunities that fit their personal interest profile. Based on this knowledge, students formulate their ninth-grade academic program.

Students and their parents first learn about ICEP when they visit Crete-Monee during the spring of their sixth-grade year. In seventh grade, students explore their interests through exercises designed to make them aware of their personal traits and interests. Students also assess their work habits and link each course they take to occupational possibilities that intrigue them. Each exercise aims to broaden, rather than narrow, students' thinking about the possibilities the future might hold.

Focusing on their futures. In the eighth grade, learning activities become more focused on gathering information, with students identifying questions to ask, locating sources of new information, and interviewing techniques. Students research basic information about occupations — salaries, benefits, and educational requirements — and align it with their personal goals. They learn how different occupations affect lifestyle, self-development, and family life as well as how personality traits, values, and interests are linked to specific occupations. A computerized career assessment and planning program pinpoints occupations related to their preferences in school subjects, abilities, lifestyles, and values. Interviews with individuals from various occupations further expose students to the world of work.

Finally, students learn specific decision-making strategies to link what they have learned about themselves and various occupations with high school course plans. During the second semester of eighth grade, students develop a four-year plan for high school. In the process of discussing high school registration requirements, students learn about graduation requirements, course levels, and the consequences of weighted grades. Teachers pay attention to the importance of course sequences and review skills necessary for success after graduation.

ICEP's program design means no student leaves the eighth grade without knowing that postsecondary training — whether it is acquired through on-the-job training, apprenticeships, trade school, community college, or four-year college — is critical to future opportunity. As counselors Ronald Allen and Debbie Hart say, "At our school, it's not an option not to plan. We tell the students what their choices mean. If they set their sights low, we tell them the consequences."

Crete-Monee's counselors and their colleagues in other untracked schools emphasize that by enabling students to research and plan their futures, they are supporting the broader goals of untracking in junior high and senior high school. The program's results back them up. Increasing numbers of graduating eighth-graders are enrolling in higher level ninth-grade courses. For example, compared with 1988 graduates, the number of 1991 graduates entering low-level courses in the ninth grade dropped by more than half, with corresponding increases in college preparatory course enrollment.

CHAPTER 4:
INGREDIENTS FOR CHANGE

How do schools trade tracking and rigid ability grouping for classroom practices that put learning for all students at the center of schooling?

The actual process of dismantling a rigid tracking system and adopting alternatives follows no prescribed recipe. Instead, untracking requires certain basic ingredients that each school uses in different proportions, measuring each according to the taste of its community, to create a flavor uniquely its own.

A Complex Process

Few schools, even those grounded in the deepest commitments to democratic schooling, have untracked completely. Why? Schools inhabit the real world with all its cultural norms and political realities, and a variety of "real world" constraints may slow or inhibit reform. Some of the constraints are budgetary or contractual. Others are political or regulatory, as is the case when state regulations mandate special or separate classes for "gifted" or "ungifted" students. Integrated classes also may seem especially daunting in communities with high rates of immigration or transience.

Untracking engages different actors, reaches different stages within varying time periods, strikes different compromises with the constituency groups, and begins at different points according to conditions in each school. For example, some schools may begin with as many as 15 different levels in all subjects and reduce that number to three. Others may start with three to five groupings and narrow that number to one or at most two instructional levels.

As these examples suggest, dismantling tracking involves far more than simply regrouping students or substituting one curriculum or instructional strategy for another. As University of Miami researcher Jeannie Oakes insists, untracking requires changes not only in teaching and learning but also in political relationships and the school culture. Some of the conditions necessary to make these changes happen include:

* School-based leadership with teacher and parent support for change.
* Ample time provided for staff development.
* A multiyear plan for change.
* Phase-in implementation by grade, team, or department.
* A hospitable policy context.

Each of these conditions contributes to the eventual success of the untracking process.

School-Based Leadership

Untracking can be an uphill battle in any school where the principal and teachers are unwilling to work together for change. The principal-teacher partnership sets the pace and scope of untracking.

Principals pave the way

In untracked schools, principals understand that their leadership responsibility is pivotal. As Janet Altersitz, principal of Desert Sky Middle School in Glendale, Arizona, warns:

Little will happen without the principal's interest, active participation, and leadership. It will be the principal's enthusiasm and modeling that will gain the attention and respect of faculty members. Soliciting appropriate funds, reviewing test data, and keeping various publics informed are key duties for the principal.

Leadership for untracking requires articulating the school's mission and communicating research-based knowledge to teachers, parents, and school board members while understanding their various perspectives. For example, Sue Galletti, principal of Lake Stevens, Washington, Middle School, remarks:

I have become increasingly convinced that understanding the context within which arguments are presented (by thoroughly understanding both points of view) is more important for creating a change than being able to articulate only one point of view.

Many shoes to fill. Principals in untracking schools also must be instructional leaders familiar with learning theory and innovative strategies for mixed-level groups. They must be available to help teachers develop professional skills and expertise. Principals of untracking schools cite the need for vision, courage, persistence, patience, and willingness to take risks. Margaret Bray, principal of Ferndale Middle School in High Point, North Carolina, summarizes the experience of other principals in untracking schools when she says, "One must be both an idealist and a pragmatist to make untracking work."

Many principals lead untracking efforts by establishing practices that promote teacher success in heterogeneous classrooms. For Christine Rath, principal of Concord High School in Concord, New Hampshire, leadership meant giving teachers common planning time where they could share successful strategies. Principals also can give teachers flexible schedules that foster professional conversations and decision making.

Teachers willing to take risks

Supportive school leadership must be combined with teacher commitment to introduce change. Principal Bray notes that untracking schools need "at least several *convinced* teachers and some teachers trained as 'in-house experts' on workable techniques."

Jake Burks, associate superintendent of Harford County Public Schools in Bel Air, Maryland, adds that involving teachers requires a school climate that both encourages risk taking and stimulates dissatisfaction with the status quo. He advises:

"One must be both an idealist and a pragmatist to make untracking work."

You need a lot of teacher collegiality and support to make this work. It's especially important to establish a climate that allows teachers to take risks. Teachers in our school were totally safe in trying different things. We also spent a lot of time on study and inquiry. Meaningful change won't occur until the people involved experience dissonance between what we know from research and what we're doing that might be the opposite.

Teachers themselves recognize that their commitment and willingness to experiment and their involvement in planning for change is crucial to success. In response to a 1991 survey on the untracking process, teachers from the Graham and Parks School in Cambridge, Massachusetts, noted:

> Untracking alone does not solve anything. It's what happens with kids after mixed-ability grouping occurs that matters. This must be put into teachers' hands — by empowering them, having them critically examine the current program, investigate other schools through visits or reading, and then develop their own ways.

Parents Support Changes

Engaging parents as powerful allies in the untracking process is usually one of the first challenges teachers and principals face. Parents with children who are in "special" programs are especially sensitive to changes in grouping. For example, parents of children with disabilities may fear heterogeneous grouping will overwhelm their children or result in less attention to their individual learning needs. On the other side are parents of children labeled "gifted," who fear that changes will result in fewer challenges for their children or undermine their children's chances to succeed.

In many schools, adopting alternatives to tracking has required educating parents about relevant research and new approaches to curriculum and instruction. Schools must persuade parents that untracking strengthens the mainstream of the school so that all students will master complex material. Principals and teachers are called on to demonstrate that students have more to gain from learning together than from learning apart in separate, labeled programs. Moreover, once untracking begins, schools must sustain parents' support.

Winning over "gifted" parents

In communities where educators are moving to heterogeneous grouping to realize a broader school vision, the most vocal opponents often are parents who expect their children to enter selective programs for "gifted and talented" students. These parents can be politically powerful and use sophisticated arguments against heterogeneous grouping. The challenge is to help them understand that inclusive schooling offers all students the type of education usually reserved for "gifted" students.

Sue Galletti, now principal of Lake Stevens Middle School in Washington, describes her experience from when she was the principal of Islander Middle School in Mercer Island, Washington:

> *Schools must persuade parents that untracking strengthens the mainstream of the school so that all students will master complex material.*

Our school was in a district where test scores were significantly higher than [those of] other districts in the state. Our parents were all college-educated, and they were very committed to sorting kids into gifted programs. When our school made the commitment to more inclusive programs, some of our parents were sophisticated enough to counter all our arguments with their own about why certain children needed to be separated into gifted classrooms. At the time, we had about 10 percent of our students in gifted classes, and we used a variety of measures to put them there...We required students to have an I.Q. score of 130, and we used this marker plus achievement scores on subtests to arrive at a total score for identifying "gifted" students.

We had lots of parent meetings, but this did not work effectively to convince parents to abandon the program. Finally, we called in a group of 30 parents who were most vocal against eliminating separate gifted programs. We met in the library, and we gave them the sixth-grade test data that we used to select students for the gifted classes for 250 real live kids. Their task was to identify 26 students for the gifted program. The parents quickly realized that 55 of these students had an IQ of 130 or above, but one student had an IQ of 150 but would not qualify because of his achievement scores and another had an IQ of 129 but did qualify once achievement scores were included. When the parents realized that they couldn't make decisions, they began to ask to expand the gifted program. I explained that even with an expanded program, I knew how some of the students would rank, and that many of the parents in the room had children who would not qualify.

At that point, the whole tenor in the room changed, and I saw lots of nonverbal reaction. We then began one hour of serious conversation, and those parents walked out of that meeting understanding that what they needed was a "gifted" program for 100 percent of the kids. At the time, that meant a "Humanities" program with integrated instruction, cooperative learning, and a focus on thinking skills. The parents decided they would go to the school board with this idea, and I thought the community was going to massacre us. But they didn't. They lauded us and the proposal as the only way to go! We still identified "top" kids by IQ, but it was used purely to make sure that we spread those students around into different working groups. And the parents are very happy with what we have done.

Another strategy for winning over skeptical parents is to have them attend professional development programs where they learn about teaching and learning in heterogeneous classes. Or, principals might invite interested parents to meet with teachers prior to implementing grouping changes. Such meetings might take the form of large forums, one-on-one meetings, or neighborhood "coffees" in the homes of PTO or school board members. These meetings benefit parents when they focus on the learning expectations that will apply to all students.

Addressing other concerns. Educators try to demonstrate that all children will gain from untracking, and no one will lose learning opportunities. For example, Jericho, New York, Middle School Principal Anna Hunderfund assured parents concerned about the elimination of the school's pull-out "gifted-and-talented" program that nothing would be taken away from their children. Instead, she explained how changes in the nine-period day would allow all students to experience the enrichment curriculum formerly offered only to a few students.

Hunderfund and others emphasize that winning parents' trust may take months or even years — and staff must be able to deliver on the promises they make. To do just that, Montclair, New Jersey, high school English teachers have hosted a series of three evening seminars.

Parents attending the seminars experience the same collaborative learning and performance assessment activities as their children in heterogeneous ninth-grade classes. They leave with greater appreciation for the rich content and pedagogy of these classes. Moreover, they see for themselves how teachers address classroom differences of students.

Finally, some schools like Kammerer Middle School in Louisville, Kentucky, introduce heterogeneous grouping as a "pilot project." They pioneer new grouping practices in one part of the school, and let experienced and enthusiastic teachers shepherd the project. By introducing heterogeneous grouping in tandem with a challenging curriculum and hands-on learning activities, such schools present parents with an educational offer so attractive that grouping concerns become secondary to the appeal of what happens in the classrooms. Ultimately, Kammerer has found the demand for the heterogeneous program is so great that the school plans to blend classes in other teams.

Professional Development and Support

S taff development for teachers is essential for successful untracking. In fact, asked what they might do differently if they were to begin again, many principals emphasize, "More staff development!" In particular, many stress the need to provide teachers with more direct exposure to learning theory and classroom techniques on teaching heterogeneous groups. In untracking schools, professional development takes three major forms:

1. Staff development to plan for whole-school change and strengthen organizational structures. Activities promote risk-taking and ongoing planning, including attention to teachers' beliefs about the nature of intelligence and the capacity of their students and colleagues to embrace more challenging learning and teaching activities.

2. Training in effective classroom instructional strategies for helping diverse students meet standards in content areas.

3. Teacher development related to implementing specific curricula that is new to the school and its teachers.

Within this framework, teachers in untracking schools may participate in professional development to:

* Build skills in participatory planning and team building;

* Review methods for communicating high expectations to all students;

* Discuss research on cognitive development and multiple intelligences;

* Develop skills in mastery learning, cooperative learning, complex instruction, Socratic dialogue, and writing across the curriculum;
* Implement a "high content" curriculum; and
* Design assessments that accurately reflect curriculum.

Build from discussions. In many untracking schools, professional development begins with teachers discussing core beliefs about learning. For example, Wellesley Middle School geared much of its professional development toward helping teachers rethink an unstated but accepted belief that some teachers were more capable of teaching certain kinds of children.

First, staff development focused on developing teachers' commitment to and capacity for teaching all students. During weekly meetings before and after school, staff familiarized themselves with research on tracking, expectations and motivation theory, and cooperative learning.

As the school phased in heterogeneous grouping, teachers tried out new techniques and approaches. Underlying this strategy was the understanding that if risk-taking was a trait the school wanted to encourage in students, the climate in the school needed to reflect that. Teachers had to take risks themselves as part of their own learning about working with different groups of students.

Support risk-taking

Beyond specific initiatives, staff development efforts establish a safe, professional climate that allows teachers to flounder as they try new approaches in heterogeneous classes. As Pep Jewell, principal of Helena, Montana, Middle School remarks:

> Inservice is an investment in the experienced professional. A professional growth strand as part of the evaluation process gives teachers permission to take the risk to be less than perfect in trying something new. Student- and teacher-teaming during the process gives support.

Such risk-taking is evident in the experimentation that occurs when schools adopt a vision of deeper, more meaningful learning for all students. For example, at San Jose's Burnett Academy, teacher Connie Posner began experimenting on her own with untracking in her English as a Second Language (ESL) classes. Instead of creating low, medium, and high groups, Posner worked with the administration and mixed the three groups. She found that all of the students progressed more rapidly and were able to enter regular classes more quickly.

Beyond specific initiatives, staff development efforts establish a safe, professional climate that allows teachers to flounder as they try new approaches in heterogeneous classes.

Determined to "make things more exciting" for all students and for herself, another Burnett teacher, Kris Estrada, assigned challenging, relevant, and empowering projects to all students. One of her colleagues, Steve Novotny, also realized that he was giving students in his "lower" classes less exciting opportunities and experiences in the computer lab. He started assigning the "fun, challenging" projects in programming and robotics to the "lower" students and was thrilled by the positive results.

Structural changes

Many principals and teachers also highlight the importance of reforming school structures that support teachers' working together to "own" curriculum and instruction. For example, Chris Lim and Ann Hiyakumoro, principal and project director of Willard Junior High School in Berkeley, California, cite the need for "wiping out teacher isolation in the school building." They say additional support for teachers is crucial "in every way possible, including extra preparation periods, paid curriculum development time, paid staff development time, good materials, and tutors for students."

At San Jose's Burnett Academy, math teachers revised their program to ensure that all students succeed in algebra before they complete the eighth grade. Burnett sixth-graders now are enrolled in heterogeneous accelerated math classes, while all seventh- graders take pre-algebra, and eighth-graders take Algebra I.

Intensive training

In untracking schools, staff development often is intensive, especially in the early stages of change. For example, in Louisville, Kentucky, teachers at three middle schools have come to prefer one- or two-week summer institutes over six- or twelve-hour workshops. They also have learned that when teams of teachers from each school rather than individuals attend such training, they are more likely to implement new classroom strategies during the subsequent school year.

Professional development in untracking schools also includes study groups, all-day training, staff retreats, visits to other schools, modeling, peer coaching, and consultations. For example, at Vermont's Rutland Middle School, all staff participated in a focused series of professional workshops paid for by the district and designed to meet a schoolwide goal of heterogeneous grouping by 1993. This goal, in turn, dovetailed with state goals to educate all children, including students with disabilities, in inclusive classrooms. Rutland teachers also attended the University of Vermont's Middle Level Summer Institute where they planned how to implement heterogeneous grouping and special education inclusion at their own grade level as these practices were phased in over three years.

When conditions in a school support teacher discussion, professional collegiality, and teamwork, staff development becomes an accepted part of the school culture.

Finding resources for staff development. In Lowell, Massachusetts, the Bartlett School adopted a different strategy for change in grades K-8. It used funds from the state's dropout prevention program to hire a "Change Facilitator" who worked directly with teachers, arranged for teacher visits to other schools, identified innovative programs, and helped teachers assess whether such programs could be incorporated at Bartlett.

Other schools have turned to resources from professional associations such as the American Association of School Administrators and the Association for Supervision and Curriculum Development. Forming partnerships with local colleges and universities is another way to introduce staff to faculty who are knowledgeable about innovative practices.

When conditions in a school support teacher discussion, professional collegiality, and teamwork, staff development becomes an accepted part of the school culture. New norms reinforce teachers as professionals who must keep up with current issues in their field and whose commitment obligates them to uphold high standards. In this context, practice must be learner-centered and reflect the most current research in the field.

Districtwide Commitment

In some cases, an entire school district commits to preparing teachers for untracking. For example, the Springfield, Massachusetts, Public Schools has worked closely with the Efficacy Institute and Research for Better Teaching, two independent staff development groups in that state. These groups have introduced educators to new intelligence models so that teachers will be stimulated to think about how they will change practice to improve learning for all students.

Over several years, all administrative staff, including principals, assistant principals, counselors, and the majority of teachers have participated in focused summer learning opportunities to develop both the philosophical foundation for teaching all students at challenging levels and a repertoire of skills that boost achievement. As Superintendent Peter Negroni explains, "You have to attach professional development to an inclusive philosophy. Inclusion is not a model; it's a value."

Further professional development is school-based, with weekly time set aside for teacher meetings approved through union negotiations. Negroni emphasizes that these times are essential for teachers to reflect, inquire, and analyze new ways of thinking, including thinking about themselves as learners. He asks:

If all kids can learn, why can't all adults learn? I hear people who say all children can learn; then they themselves say they can't do something. It's so obvious we limit ourselves. Professionals have to take responsibility for learning. We can't refuse to do the things that will help us learn.

Staff development principles

The professional development experiences of untracking schools reflect many of the principles for successful professional development proposed by the National Staff Development Council. However, Dennis Sparks, NSDC executive director, explains:

The hard part is getting people ready to say "OK, what do we need to do differently now?" So it's important to provide lots of opportunities for staff to talk about what they believe and how it relates to classroom practice. Unless people get the chance to construct their own meaning in the process of change, it's likely their current beliefs will remain in place.

Sparks also emphasizes several staff development principles that relate to untracking:

* School-based staff development makes sense. Staff development should involve everyone in the school — support staff, office staff, custodians — not just teachers.

* Staff development should be job-embedded. "In the best of all possible worlds, every educator would be part of study teams doing action research, watching peers, discussing what is happening in a classroom, and jointly planning and writing new curriculum. These things make it virtually impossible to hide outmoded practices," he says.

* Good staff development requires ongoing follow-up through on-the-job coaching and continuous discussions. Continual school renewal becomes the norm.

Above all, says Sparks, staff development has to be directed toward improved student performance. He notes, "Satisfaction and exposure are not enough. Staff development has to be the means to success for all kids."

Planning for Change

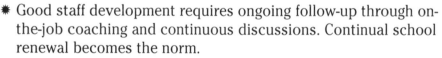

Successful untracking depends on planning for change, a process that builds teacher commitment to untracking. Planning requires putting aside time for a representative group of teachers to work with administrators to debate and discuss new routines, schedules,

teaching approaches, curricula, and relationships. Planning in these groups may be schoolwide, in each grade or department, or in a teacher team within the larger school.

Broad agreement and involvement

If successful planning for untracking begins with broad agreement about the school's mission, it continues by involving all participants — teachers, parents, and administrators — in thinking about what they expect all students leaving their school to know and be able to do. School staff also review data regularly to determine how close they are to realizing these goals. Over time, the attention to comparing "where we are" with "where we want to be" becomes a habit among all members of the school community.

> "*We question practically everything. We ask whether our practices align with research, and when we find gaps, we work team by team to figure out action plans to close them.*"

Change participants are especially attuned to recent findings of educational research. Susan Masek, principal of Sierra Middle School in Tucson, Arizona, explains, "We set out to adopt the practices known to benefit our students. Heterogeneous grouping was one of those."

As teachers learn to apply research to school practices, they become accustomed to inquiry. Sandra Caldwell, principal of the Middle School for the Kennebunks in Kennebunkport, Maine, reports, "We question practically everything. We ask whether our practices align with research, and when we find gaps, we work team by team to figure out action plans to close them."

Working toward a vision. In short, untracking is a school-culture norm, not a one-shot event. It is a continuous, problem-solving process that involves developing a vision, gathering data and research, setting targets, and finally revisiting the vision.

Some schools begin their planning with an "awareness raising" period, during which principals provide staff with data, and teachers read current research articles related to tracking and cognitive development. During this time, teachers often visit heterogeneous classrooms in other schools, form school-based study groups to research specific grouping and curriculum changes, make decisions about new directions, and plan further staff development to ensure that these changes are effective.

Whatever the model, the untracking process takes place over several years, sometimes spanning five to eight years. However, while some schools that initiated grouping changes in the early or mid-1980s have taken up to eight years to untrack, principals of these same schools now emphasize that untracking doesn't need to take so long.

"We now have much better evidence documenting the harm of tracking," says Janet Altersitz, principal of Desert Sky Middle School in Glendale, Arizona. Desert Sky dismantled more than 30 instructional levels during a seven-year period. She adds, "Given what we know from research and the resources now available to develop alternative approaches to curriculum and instruction, schools should be able to make great gains in three years."

Phasing In Changes

As already stated, successful untracking does not happen overnight. While untracking schools accept change as a norm, they make changes systematically, often introducing heterogeneous grouping, new curricula, and diverse instructional techniques in stages. They follow no formula. However, schools typically phase in changes one grade, department, cluster, or team at a time.

Sandra Caldwell, principal of Maine's Middle School of the Kennebunks, explains:

You have to understand that different people have different comfort levels. We don't expect everyone to do everything at the same time. We have always, with everything, piloted with teachers who felt comfortable. We have never made major changes overnight, but we need to allow people who are ready to go ahead.

Peeling off the bottom levels. As a first step, schools often reduce the number of instructional levels in most disciplines, first by folding the lower levels into the middle levels. Many untracked schools initially eliminated homogeneously grouped classes in social studies and science. After a few years, many virtually eliminated reading and language arts levels, but most still offered two or three levels in math. And some schools went even further, introducing totally nongraded arrangements. In Kentucky, for example, legislation now mandates nongraded groupings before fourth grade.

In addition, peeling off the bottom tracks can bring the unexpected benefit of freeing teachers who have worked exclusively with remedial, Chapter 1, or special education classes to work in heterogeneous classrooms, either on their own or paired with other teachers.

For example, in Wellesley, once the school found that lower-scoring students could succeed in grade-level classes, teachers formerly assigned to the "low" classes were available to co-teach in multiability classrooms. So even though students in these classes had to master more complex material than they were accustomed to, they also had the resource of an extra teacher to support them.

Begin in the early grades. Untracking efforts in a school's earliest grades often support changes in subsequent grades. For example, when Muirlands Middle School in LaJolla, California, made the transition from a traditional junior high to a middle school, sixth-grade teachers insisted on teaching heterogeneous groups of students in science and the humanities as if all students were "gifted and talented."

Empowered with skills developed through training in the Council for Basic Education's Writing To Learn program and through their association with Harvard University's Performance Assessment Collaborative Education project, Muirlands teachers offered all students a challenging, high content curriculum. Courses blended students of all abilities and broke down tracks that had clearly separated students by race.

After one year, teachers compared students' fifth-grade standardized test scores with their scores at the end of sixth grade. The results were compelling. Not only had the lowest scoring students moved from the bottom into the middle deciles; scores of the top achievers in the heterogeneous classes had not suffered. Armed with these data, sixth-grade teachers persuaded their seventh-grade colleagues to maintain heterogeneous groupings in their grade for all subjects except math. Following the example of teachers in these two grades, eighth-grade teachers at Muirlands are now poised to continue the success of the earlier two grades.

Supporting Policies

Untracking begins at the school level, but some schools do not have the resources or clout to "go it alone." In these cases, a district or state policy can reinforce progress, provide a cushion of support, and establish a broader climate for change.

However, a mere paper policy discouraging tracking is not enough to put an end to harmful grouping practices. The formal message of a policy advisory, position statement, or implementation guidelines from key decision makers creates the climate that tolerates difficult changes — and makes life easier for innovators at the school level. As Deborah Meier, co-director of New York's Central Park East Secondary School, notes:

> What the "system" can do is create the structural conditions that encourage people to want to change and give them sufficient autonomy to do so, and that provide support and encouragement even when they blunder in the course of creating their interpretation of the "good school." But in the end, the change must be home-grown. While some untracking schools get needed support from their district offices and school boards, many successfully adopt new grouping, instruction, and curricula within the context of broader school reform movements of the 1980s. Whatever the context, the sense of belonging to a larger network, along with technical assistance, provides schools with a friendly environment to begin change.

District-level policy

In Burlington, Vermont, Monica Nelson, director of curriculum, says the school board's curriculum committee spent one full year reviewing research on tracking and discussing the pros and cons of student grouping practices. From this dialogue, the board adopted the curriculum committee's "Grouping Motion" in March 1991, allowing Burlington's two middle schools to develop their own individualized plans for untracking over a three-year period.

Burlington's policy recognizes schools will be ready for change at different times. In addition, the Grouping Motion includes directions to the board, the superintendent, and the curriculum director supporting schools' untracking efforts. It also requires each school to submit an initial action plan that addresses alternatives to ability grouping.

The policy also established a three-year time frame for implementing heterogeneous grouping — a goal principals must account for in their school plans. Educators who don't want to become involved in untracking may try to delay the process as long as possible. As Nelson explains, "I told the curriculum committee, 'A small but vocal group will always think this is the pits…If you really want anything to happen, you need to set a date.'"

State-level policy

State-level policy statements also create momentum for untracking. In Massachusetts, the State Board of Education's 1990 policy advisory, *Structuring Schools for Student Success: A Focus on Ability Grouping*, set the stage for local school reform. Two years later, 69 percent of the state's middle grades principals reported a decrease in tracking and an increase in heterogeneous grouping. A current state law requiring all schools to abolish the "general track" is expected to stimulate further changes.

Policies are only the beginning. The most important feature of the Massachusetts policy is the state's commitment to provide concrete resources to schools, especially those in high poverty districts, that adopt heterogeneous grouping. Dan French, director of the education department's division of instructional services grants, says:

We do know that heterogeneous grouping has a more positive impact on student achievement than homogeneous grouping. Since we want to tie our funding to educational approaches that work, we direct our resources to schools that are working to adopt good practice. In awarding both dropout and remedial grants, we've included heterogeneous grouping of students as one of our required objectives.

In addition to grants, Massachusetts also provides on-site technical assistance and professional development opportunities to schools adopting heterogeneous grouping. This assistance might involve statewide conferences, regional seminars, and the pairing of schools working on grouping issues with others who may be "a little further along."

"Many districts need incentives to try something new, especially if it's controversial," French says. "A state policy promoting heterogeneous grouping can supply a necessary safety net for districts willing to take the risk, but linking resources to change is what really boosts the credibility of the effort."

Funding for professional development, allocated as part of Massachusetts' recently enacted education reform legislation, will continue to support such changes.

Broad-based change. In California, a broad initiative directed at reforming the state's middle level schools provides the context for untracking. In 1987, *Caught in the Middle*, a report published by the California Department of Education recommended substantially reducing tracking. The report advised against tracking students in grades 6, 7, and 8 according to their ethnicity, gender, general ability, primary language, or handicap. Other recommendations dealt with curriculum, instructional practice, academic counseling, "at-risk" students, and staff development.

The report also established a vehicle for transforming the reform agenda into practice: a partnership of local school districts, institutions of higher education, and the California Department of Education to develop 100 state-of-the-art middle schools to catalyze reform throughout the state.

In response, the Office of Middle Grades Support Services at the California Department of Education invited all middle-level schools to participate in regional networks, each comprising ten "membership" schools and a lead or "foundation" school. Within each network, schools reviewed the findings of *Caught in the Middle*. Then they selected the recommended reforms they would pursue in their individual schools, with the support of their network. This reform process reinforced principles of local control and mutual collaboration for school improvement.

From the beginning, the networks honed in on issues of untracking and equal opportunity. Through monthly principals' meetings at rotated sites, visits to "sister schools," newsletters, directories, telecommunications networks, and collaborative staff development days, schools shared strategies for realizing the goals of heterogeneous grouping and curriculum reform. In addition, a summer symposium on "Equal Access" featured workshops on expanding access of low-income and ethnic minority students to the highest and most valuable middle grades curricula.

Again, belonging to a larger network of schools encouraged principals to take risks. "The Partnership gave me the courage to speak out," explains Donald LeMay of Valley Junior High School in Carlsbad, California. "It put me in contact with others who were thinking along similar lines. It gave me leverage to be able to say to skeptics in my district that we were not alone."

CONCLUSION

In response to new research, social conditions, and community pressures, schools are reviewing their current tracking and ability grouping practices with an eye toward how they affect student learning. As schools reconsider these practices, they are discovering that these outmoded practices stand in the way of their highest aspirations for student learning. Thus, many schools are developing and adapting new classroom strategies to engage all children in meaningful learning.

Schools that have started the untracking journey have seen student achievement and self-esteem rise, especially among students formerly placed in low or average groups. Classroom and school climate are greatly improved as discipline problems decline. Teachers are working harder, but many are invigorated in unexpected ways as they renew a commitment to their own learning.

Untracking schools do not all face the same challenges. The route each takes depends on the resources available and the terrain that must be covered in a difficult but worthwhile journey. In all cases, however, sufficient training and resources must be provided to enable teachers and other staff to take risks in a safe environment.

Complementary goals

New student groupings force everyone to confront an essential question: How can our public schools teach all students at high levels? As schools and communities work to answer that question, they must engage the bored and unmotivated students who are typically neglected in the low and average groups. But they also must challenge the most confident students. Overcoming this challenge means improved teaching and learning for everyone — the ultimate promise of untracking. In addressing the imperative for equity, untracking schools find excellence. In finding excellence, they realize equity.

GLOSSARY

Ability Grouping: The practice of sorting students, particularly during elementary and middle school, into classes or work groups based on their perceived ability levels (average, below average, above average). Students in different classes typically are exposed to different curricula and instruction. (See also *tracking*.)

Authentic Instruction: A general term for a method of alternative instruction that focuses on increasing students' problem-solving abilities in "real-life" situations. Common features of authentic instruction include an emphasis on developing students' higher order thinking skills, increasing their depth of knowledge, connecting classwork and subjects to the world, encouraging substantive conversation of issues being studied, and providing needed social supports for student achievement.

Between-Class Grouping: The practice of grouping students with similar abilities into separate classes for the purpose of providing them with instruction targeted to their perceived abilities. (See also *whole-class grouping*.)

Complex Instruction: A teaching approach that aims to improve the achievement of children who frequently are subject to lower expectations because of their ethnicity, socioeconomic status, perceived ability, or other factors. Complex instruction frequently uses heterogeneous groupings, cooperative learning, and multiple-intelligence theory to engage all students in a rich problem-solving, project-based curriculum.

Cooperative Learning: A partner- or group-based instructional method where students work together on a project or assignment, with an emphasis on cooperation and team learning. The students, who usually have varying abilities and backgrounds, assume well-defined roles as they work to complete the assignment.

Curriculum Differentiation: The practice of using different objectives, techniques, and instructional materials to organize curriculum with different groups of students, according to their apparent academic ability.

Flexible Grouping: The practice of grouping for temporary, skill-specific learning used in many untracking classrooms.

Gifted and Talented: Selective programs to provide advanced or accelerated instruction to a group of students identified — usually through standardized testing — as having high or above-average ability. Separate gifted and talented programs for specific students contradict the central belief in untracking schools that all children are gifted in different ways — and that all children should have access to stimulating, challenging instruction, with appropriate support.

Heterogeneous Grouping: A method of grouping students with varying abilities, learning styles, backgrounds, and racial and ethnic groups in the same classes or work groups, with an emphasis on challenging curriculum and instruction for all students. Educators who practice heterogeneous grouping believe the diversity in their classes benefits every student and ensures equal access to valued knowledge.

Higher Order Thinking Skills: The application and reasoning skills needed to think creatively and solve problems in academic content areas. These skills go beyond rote memorization of facts and formulas.

Homogeneous Grouping: The practice of grouping students with the same perceived ability or performance levels (low, average, high) in the same classes and work groups. Homogeneous grouping is based on the premise that students of like abilities will work better if they are grouped together, and the teacher can target instruction to their abilities. In reality, this practice often results in large groups of students, particularly those labeled low or average, being tracked into the same ability groups and classes throughout their school careers.

Inclusion: The practice of bringing students who traditionally are taught in separate classes or programs, such as special education, disabled, and other students with special learning needs, into the general education classroom for all or most of their instruction. Appropriate in-class assistance from special education teachers and aides is available.

Multiple Intelligences: A theory that suggests students learn and work in a variety of ways, such as through verbal, mathematical, or hands-on activities. Different types of intelligence are valued as legitimate ways of reaching understanding of concepts and ideas. Intelligences can also be developed through classroom learning activities and interaction. In many untracking schools, instruction and other classroom practices address the different intelligences and learning styles of students. Harvard psychologist Howard Gardner identified seven intelligences in his well-known book, *Frames of Mind:* linguistic, logical, musical, spatial, bodily/kinesthetic, interpersonal, and intrapersonal.

Nongraded Grouping: Term used to describe schools or classes that group children together during the primary or elementary school years, without concern for their age or what grade the child is in, such as first, second, or third grade (not to be confused with the elimination of letter grades).

Outcome-Based Education: An educational philosophy that identifies specific skills all students need to know and be able to do as well as strategies for students to meet them. OBE stresses that all students can and need to meet agreed-upon levels of proficiency, given flexible time and support to do so. Frequently, untracking schools also are involved in outcome-based education efforts.

Pull-Out Program: An instructional approach that removes certain groups of students from the larger, "regular" classroom for separate instruction in a different setting. Chapter 1, special education, and disabled students frequently are taught in pull-out programs. Although some untracking schools may use pull-out programs, they are intended as temporary measures to help special groups of students develop needed skills to excel in challenging heterogeneous classes.

Thematic Curriculum: An approach to organizing learning that motivates students to investigate interesting ideas from multiple perspectives. The central theme becomes the catalyst for understanding concepts, generalizations, skills, and perceptions. These themes may be broad-based or narrow in scope; may be used in designated classes or schoolwide; and may last for a few weeks, several months, or an entire semester.

Tracking: The practice of sorting students, particularly during middle and high school, into different classes (low, average, high) or courses of study (college preparatory, vocational, general) based on educators' judgments of students' intellectual abilities, prior performance, or predictions of students' future accomplishments. Students in different classrooms are exposed to different curricula and instruction. (See also *ability grouping*.)

Untracking: The process of eliminating rigid student groupings based on perceived academic abilities and predicted future accomplishments. Instead, untracking schools group students with different abilities, learning styles, and backgrounds in the same classes — with appropriate support — guaranteeing all students access to the same knowledge and opportunities.

Within-Class Grouping: An alternative to tracking, these student groupings are flexible, temporary, skill-specific, and designed to support students' success in heterogeneous classes that emphasize challenging curricula and instruction.

Whole-Class Ability Grouping: A characteristic of tracked schools, this type of grouping sorts students by ability level into separate classes for particular academic subjects. Thus, all average students are in the same class and have no interaction with above-average or below-average students in that subject area. (See also *between-class grouping*.)

ESOURCES

Bellanca, James and Swartz, Elizabeth (eds.) *The Challenge of Detracking: A Collection.* Palatine, IL: IRI/Skylight Publishing (1993).

Brooks, Jacqueline Grennon and Brooks, Martin G. *In Search of Understanding: The Case for Constructivist Classrooms.* Alexandria, VA: Association for Supervision and Curriculum Development (1993).

Cohen, Elizabeth. *Designing Groupwork: Strategies for the Heterogeneous Classroom.* New York, NY: Teachers' College Press (1987).

Common Destiny Alliance. *Realizing Our Nation's Diversity as an Opportunity: Alternatives To Sorting America's Children.* Nashville, TN: Vanderbilt Institute for Public Policy Studies (1992).

Gardner, Howard. *Frames of Mind.* New York, NY: Basic Books (1983).

Goodlad, John I. *A Place Called School: Prospects for the Future.* New York, NY: McGraw-Hill (1984).

Oakes, Jeannie. *Keeping Track: How Schools Structure Inequality.* New Haven, CT: Yale University Press (1985).

Oakes, Jeannie and Lipton, Martin. *Making the Best of Schools: A Handbook for Parents, Teachers, and Policymakers.* New Haven, CT: Yale University Press (1990).

Wheelock, Anne. *Crossing the Tracks: How "Untracking" Can Save America's Schools.* New York, NY: New Press (1992).

ACKNOWLEDGMENTS

The author, Anne Wheelock, is an education policy fellow at Northeastern University in Boston, Massachusetts. She is an education writer who has studied tracking issues extensively.

Ms. Wheelock used research conducted for her 1992 book, ***Crossing the Tracks: How "Untracking" Can Save America's Schools,*** as the foundation for this new publication. She has updated and expanded on much of the information through surveys, telephone conversations, personal interviews, and school visits. She is grateful to the many authors cited in these pages who have told the stories of their schools' journeys from structures that rested on rigid ability-grouped classes to ones that provide meaningful learning opportunities for all students.

The fundamental commitment of these educators is to ensure that public schools offer their best to all children. Although they do not have a simple blueprint for realizing the dual goals of equity and high level learning, the images of excellence they are constructing in their school communities suggest guidelines for school reform that other schools can apply.

Gary Marx, AASA senior associate executive director, served as project director. Leslie Eckard, AASA publications manager; and Katie Ross, AASA communications assistant, edited the manuscript and supervised the production process. Graphic design was provided by Dahlman/Middour Design of McLean, Virginia.